THE MONOTHEIZING PROCESS

Other Books by James A. Sanders
available from Wipf and Stock Publishers

Canon and Community
A Guide to Canonical Criticism

From Sacred Story to Sacred Text
Canon as Paradigm

God Has a Story Too
Sermons in Context

Torah and Canon
2nd ed.

The Monotheizing Process

Its Origins and Development

James A. Sanders

with a contribution from
Paul E. Capetz

CASCADE *Books* • Eugene, Oregon

THE MONOTHEIZING PROCESS
Its Origins and Development

Cascade Books
An Imprint of Wipf and Stock Publishers
199 W. 8th Ave., Suite 3
Eugene, OR 97401

www.wipfandstock.com

ISBN 13: 978-1-62564-527-2

Cataloguing-in-Publication data:

Sanders, James A., 1927–

    The monotheizing process : its origins and development / James A.
Sanders ; with a contribution by Paul E. Capetz.

    viii + 94 p. ; 23 cm. Includes bibliographical references and indexes.

    ISBN 13: 978-1-62564-527-2

    1. Bible—Old Testament—Theology. 2. Bible—New Testament—
Theology. 3. Monotheism—Israel—History. 4. Christianity and other religions.
5. Abrahamic religions. I. Capetz, Paul E. II. Title.

BS1192.6 S40 2014

Manufactured in the U.S.A.   10/22/2014

The appendix previously appeared as "Credo in Unum Deum: A Challenge." *Biblical Theology Bulletin* 39 (2009) 204–13. Used with permission.

Warm thanks for all I've learned from students,
pastors, and layfolk
during sixty years of teaching, lecturing,
and conducting pastors' schools
in the U.S. and abroad.

Contents

1

Monotheism and
the Monotheizing Process

JUDAISM, CHRISTIANITY, AND ISLAM claim to be monotheistic, but none of them actually is; none of the three has yet arrived at true monotheism the Bible and the Qur'an mandate, that is, belief in there being but One God of All. Each often claims its concept of God is the One God despite the fact that the Bible and the Qur'an insist that the true God is indefinable and incomprehensible. Many passages of the Bible are polytheistic, and yet the Judaism that emerged out of the Babylonian exile claimed to believe in One God. Reading critically, moving from the older passages through to the later, the careful reader is able to trace a process that is best called *monotheizing*. In effect the first commandment of the Decalogue, the first of Jesus's two great commandments, and the Qur'an's clear mandate fashion an imperative to continue the monotheizing process that is not yet complete but enjoins adherents of each to live life in the belief that there is but One God of All.

1

The Monotheizing Process

Enlightenment Hermeneutics

The following probe is based on the hermeneutic of the Bible and method of study associated with Enlightenment study of the Bible. *Hermeneia* in classical Greek meant "understanding." How one reads the Bible clearly depends on what one's understanding of the Bible is. In Enlightenment study, the Bible is a composite of contributions by numerous speakers, thinkers, and authors of five culture eras in antiquity over the course of two millennia—from the Late Bronze Age to the Greco-Roman era. They of necessity thought and wrote in the cultural idioms and thought-forms of their times. The method used in critical study of the Bible may be expressed by the hermeneutic triangle.

The reader is a major factor in how Scripture is read. Reading any form of literature is a dialogue between reader and text. A text is nothing but squiggles on parchment, papyrus, paper, or screen until encountered by a reader. The triangle is made up of three major aspects of that encounter: 1) the text in its complexity, created by author/s in antiquity; 2) the sociopolitical situations out of which the text arose and then was later read and reread until it achieved a stable textual form; and 3) the hermeneutic used by the various ancient contributors to the text as well as the hermeneutic of later readers.[1] All three factors must be studied carefully in order to understand first what a text is about, and then (reusing the triangle) how it was subsequently read in later situations.

In order to recover a biblical passage's original meanings, the three points of the hermeneutic triangle are all equally important.[2] The triangle is also crucial for setting aside old synagogue, mosque, and church traditions about developed meanings of their Scriptures so that the original meanings that impelled the several parts of Scripture to become parts of scriptural canons in the first place can be retrieved. The triangle also helps us retrieve later understandings of Scripture—understandings that changed with the

---

1. See Sanders, "Adaptable for Life."
2. Sanders, *Torah and Canon* (2nd ed.), 95–103.

changing needs of later generations.[3] It exposes the hermeneutic of all later readers and hearers, and how their hopes and needs in re-reading and rehearing Scripture provided the lens through which it is read. In over fifty years' study of the *Nachleben* of Scripture (passages cited, alluded to, echoed), no two bore the same meaning. "How do you effectively pass your traditions down through time? You can't just keep things as they were. Stasis is death. You have to be dynamic to survive."[4]

Monotheism?

There has been much discussion over the years about where Israel got its idea of monotheism. Egypt's religious "revolution" under Amenhotep IV (middle fourteenth century BCE) is most often credited as influencing Moses's support of the idea. The results have been less than convincing, to say the least, because the idea failed to take hold in Egypt, and the biblical text of the Torah itself is fraught with stories assuming polytheism, thus making the idea tenuous in the Torah. This has caused the field to look elsewhere for how the concept of monotheism arose in the Bible, and why.

The primary and foundational commandment in the Bible, whether the first of the Decalogue (Exod 20:2–3; Deut 5:6–7) or the first of Jesus's two commandments (Matt 22:37; Mark 12:30; Luke 10:27), is the governing concept of the Bible as a whole. The *Shema'* (Deut 6:4) that Jesus cites as the first commandment (Mark 12:29–30; Luke 10:27; Matt 22:37–38) heralded a clear step in the process that the Decalogue in the previous chapter (Deut 5:6–7) mandates. But the Josianic Reformation in the seventh century BCE, which was centered in the book of Deuteronomy, was but an internal, ecumenical movement to unify the various cults of Yahweh scattered throughout the land—a far cry from monotheism.[5]

---

3. B. A. Brown, *Three Testaments.*
4. Downey, "The Ephemeral City," 63.
5. Lange and Eshel, "The LORD is One."

The Monotheizing Process

The Bible is not itself a monotheistic literature.[6] There is no treatise in it that expounds monotheism, as one might expect, for instance, in a classical Greek document—despite the moving poetic assertions in Isaiah 40–45. On the contrary, many passages, especially in the First Testament, exhibit traits of ancient polytheism. Israel was basically polytheistic to henotheistic until the preexilic prophets were reviewed in the Babylonian exile.[7] Even to proclaim that Yahweh is One, as does the *Shema'* (Deut 6:4), which Jesus cites, is not yet full affirmation of monotheism. But read in a historical-critical mode the *Shema'* was a major étape in the monotheizing process.[8] That is, when one reads the Bible beginning with the historically older sections or passages on through the two Testaments, including the massive literature of Early Judaism, one traces a movement (bumpy for sure, and far from smooth) from polytheistic thinking through henotheistic thought (like the *Shema's* affirmation of one Yahweh) to monotheizing modes of understanding God's relation to Israel and the world beyond (especially in the classical prophets). It was when, influenced by Wisdom thinking, the prophets discerned that Yahweh was no longer just a national redeemer deity but was also the creator God of all, that new life after the death of old Israel and Judah became possible.[9] Reading the Prophetic corpus as part of the Jewish canon, or Tanakh, places it—between the story of the rise and traumatic fall of old Israel and Judah, and the collection of Early Jewish reviews of the story in the Writings—affords a clear perspective on the crucial role the monotheizing movement played in the Phoenix-like rise of Early Judaism out of the ashes of old Israel and Judah.

6. N. MacDonald, *Deuteronomy*.

7. Smith, *The Early History of God*. Polytheism indicates belief in several gods (redemptive god[s] like Yahweh in the early phases of biblical history, fertility gods, personal deities, family, or triabal gods, etc.). Henotheism indicates belief in one god per tribe or nation, or one god per religion in the current situation.

8. Sanders, *Canon and Community*, 84.

9. Sanders, "The Book of Job."

Monotheizing

Unfortunately the move from henotheistic thinking to a fully monotheizing mode of reading Scripture and thinking its thoughts (that is, from thinking of God as *our* God to thinking of *their* God being also *our* God) has been difficult for the human mind to make. The three so-called monotheistic faiths—Judaism, Christianity, and Islam—continue to think and act for the most part henotheistically. That is, each insists it is monotheistic, but each also thinks its view of God is the only correct one; and that is henotheism.[10] Tribalism, no matter how big or diverse the tribe becomes—even as big as a worldwide religion—is apparently a difficult cultural habit to break.

Monotheism as a concept has been burdened with the trappings of ancient, patriarchal cultural norms in which the Bible, of necessity, was expressed, and is sometimes denigrated or even dismissed because of those cultural traits.[11] The Bible and the Qur'an were formed and shaped in the cultural terms of the folk who wrote them. They had no alternative, just as our own reading and thinking are shaped and formed by the cultures in which we express ourselves. They, like us, lived, moved and had their beings in the cultural confines of the times in which they lived. They, like us, thought and conceived even their best thoughts in the terms they had available to them. They had and we have no other. It is extremely difficult to think outside the cultural box we inherit and inhabit even when we have studied and appreciated other languages and cultures. But God, by definition, cannot be confined to any box—even the boxes of our greatest theological thinking, especially doctrines (teachings) about God.

The Bible and the Qur'an preserve perhaps the best of ancient thought about God—thoughts that canonically spanned generational and situational gaps and spoke to more than one condition: the essence of the concept of canon.[12] The ability to span genera-

---

10. Niebuhr, *Radical Monotheism.*
11. Sanders and Capetz, *"Credo in Unum Deum."* See Appendix.
12. Sanders, "The Canonical Process."

tional and situational divides is probably the reason what is in the canon of each religion survived passing from one ancient cultural era to another. What survived and spoke to communities' needs apparently also spoke to several generations and several different cultures during which the Bible was formed, from the Late Bronze Age to the Greco-Roman. What is there was found repeatable and resourceful (that is, helpful) by later generations and communities other than those in which they were first expressed and then passed on.[13] The Bible refers directly to some thirty-two ancient literary titles[14] that did not make it into any canon. (Most of the massive amount of Jewish literature included in the so-called Pseudepigrapha also failed to make it into any canon of which we are aware.) Either what is in a canon in some measure met the needs of the communities that received it beyond the ones that created it, or it was, without malice aforethought, simply set aside and not picked up again. It was the passing on that was important; it was the acceptance by neighboring and later communities that was crucial.[15]

One God of All

The three monotheistic religions—Judaism, Christianity, and Islam—have almost totally been stuck in a henotheistic mode, each claiming that its concept of God is the one true God, but that falls far short of the monotheism each professes. Since monotheism has so far eluded the classical monotheistic religions, what is needed to revive the process is serious effort by the adherents of each to monotheize: that is, to see that all the various religions of the world are differing cultural efforts to worship the One Reality that binds us all. Religions other than the "big three" that tend toward thinking of a single deity that unifies all the minor ones they profess should not be excluded from the monotheizing conversation.

13. Sanders, *Canon and Community*, 21–45.
14. Leiman, *The Canonization of Hebrew Scripture*, 16–26.
15. Sanders, "Adaptable for Life."

Monotheism and the Monotheizing Process

To monotheize is to confess that the One God of All is beyond human ability to define or describe, and that while humans grope to understand Reality in its totality, we fall short of doing so. All humans, even those who claim to be atheist, try to grasp what it is we were thrown into in the short passage that earthly life offers from birth to death. The following words are attributed to Albert Einstein: "There is a reality beyond which human understanding in impotent and helpless. Human life is a mystery. We appear here uninvited for a short stay, then we are no more." Science, especially astrophysics, tries to plumb the mystery inductively, but fails—but should continue since its mission for being demands it continue to try to see things whole. The search for the meaning of black holes is a part of science's continuing efforts to comprehend the whole of the multiverse.

Religion and science ultimately both strive to comprehend the integrity of Reality. Scientists seem comfortable with terms like *nature* and the like, but often those terms end up where others would use *God*. Most of Western Christianity views the Holy Spirit as the liberator from the ancient cultural traps and trappings of antiquity and the spiritual force that led most churches into the Enlightenment age of science and discovery. Western Christians also view the Enlightenment as a gift of God in due season and not as God's enemy, as does static thinking. (Fundamentalists, including some who call themselves evangelicals, have limited the role of the Holy Spirit to inspiring individual Christians and hence fight vigorously against the results of the Enlightenment and science, especially the hermeneutic exhibited in this essay.[16])

The commandment that follows the first in the biblical Decalogue forbids making images of God because some ancients realized already in their time that God cannot be confined to a shape humans can imagine and fashion, hence prohibitions against "graven images" of any sort to represent God. God is indefinable and incomprehensible to both science and religion. The Integrity of Reality is beyond human ability to define, that is, to confine

16. Sanders, "The Betrayal of Evangelicalism."

to any cultural forms of thought and expression. The concept of God is beyond human grasp. The biblical prophets were almost all accused in their time of blasphemy (that is, of believing that God could not be contained in the received doctrinal boxes of their time). Religions tend to develop teachings about God, and unfortunately such doctrines tend to become old cultural boxes that confine concepts of God. God cannot be contained in any box. God is always bigger than humans can think.

But it is important not just to believe in there being but One God of all creation, incomprehensible to all. Further, it is important to act like it, to view not only God as One but all humanity as creatures of the One God, and to treat others as though of one ilk.[17]

It may be that humans will never be able to arrive fully at true monotheism. The Bible (in many places) and the Qur'an (surah 1:1, 7 et al.) in effect demand that humans engage in the striving itself, in living and acting out lives believing that Reality, including humanity, has integrity—an integrity apparently beyond human grasp. A passage that should startle every reader in every generation is embedded in Matthew's Sermon on the Mount (Matt 5:43–48; cf. Luke 6:27–31; hence in Q). Jesus there teaches that if we love our enemies and do good to those who persecute us, we may become "sons of God," that is divine beings (members of the heavenly council) ourselves. Members of the heavenly council were viewed as divine but as having no power themselves, except as commanded by the One God, whose job was to see that justice be done on earth (Psalm 82).

Jesus goes on to point out that God causes the sun and rain to pour their boon and their bane on both the evil and the good, the just and the unjust. While with our moralizing tendencies we may not like it, we must admit that that is exactly what happens. Both rain and sun bless and threaten all (whether good or evil) alike. It should also force us to ask what *good* and *evil*, *just* and *unjust*, mean, but to do so in an open search is to admit that what may seem good to our side in a dispute may seem evil to an opponent's, and vice versa. A simple proverb like "Into every life some rain

17. Capetz, "The First Commandment."

must fall" is of necessity understood in opposite ways according to where one lives. For those in green climates it means one has to be prepared for inclement weather, but in dry climates it heralds the good news that rain will eventually come to bless. At this very point in his own thinking, the exilic Isaiah pointed out that God's thoughts and ways are as different from ours as heaven is above the earth (Isa 55:8–10). That arresting thought is followed by a verse not dissimilar to the gospel message: rain and snow fall from heaven, providing boon to sower and bread to the eater—without distinguishing between good and bad sowers and eaters.

2

Monotheizing and the Canon

First Testament Problem Passages

These passages exhibit the same monotheizing thrust as a number of difficult parts of the First Testament, such as the fourteen times the book of Exodus says that God hardened the heart of Pharaoh (Exod 7:3 and elsewhere) or the command God gave the prophet Isaiah to preach so that hearts be hard and their ears deaf so that they not repent (Isa 6:9–10). How could God harden Pharaoh's heart? Why did God seem to support the enemy's point of view? Why would God command a prophet to preach so that the people would resist repentance? How can that be? Critically, it is probably to be credited originally to the simplistic belief, then and now, that if it happened, it must have been God's will. But in full historical-critical context it takes on a powerfully monotheizing thrust.

Yet, to read the text as received—that God understood Pharaoh's position, yet that God nonetheless freed the slaves—should give us profound pause. The Bible in many passages affirms that God indeed has a bias, a deep commitment to the poor and powerless. In order to address such issues, one needs to explore the nature of Scripture and its principal thrusts.

Monotheizing and the Canon

Studying the Psalms Scroll and other Psalms manuscripts from Qumran (caves 4 and 11) brought some in the field to ask a basic question: what was the canonical status of Psalms materials from Qumran either among the sect there or in Judaism generally?[1] Not long after that, it was claimed that the Temple or Torah Scroll was canonical at Qumran, one scholar suggesting that it was designed to replace the Mosaic Torah.[2]

Thinking of that basic question brought some to ask what actually is meant by *canon*.[3] It was clear from the start that there are two basic aspects to the concept, both in use at the same time: form and function, or to use the classical expressions, *norma normata* (form) and *norma normans* (function). The focus had until that time almost exclusively been on form, but most agree generally that function precedes form, and the question of what gave rise to the concept of canon inevitably arose. It had generally been taken to be the move following redaction critical activity[4] of any bloc of text as the next step in the history of the formation of the Bible, and there is some truth to that observation of canon as form (*norma normata*).[5]

But it seemed that, also because of the Scrolls, another approach was needed—one that would probe into why any piece of literature (oral or written) of any length was read again for the first time, even perhaps before the history of the formation of the text began, and was then reread by other communities in antiquity. Searches then were made for substantive material in the Bible that indicated frequent repetition before formation of a bloc of text necessarily began. One needed first to search the text of the whole First Testament for what may have been an early repeatable story or account.

1. Goshen-Gottstein, "The Psalms Scroll"; Sanders, "Cave 11 Surprises."

2. Wacholder, *Dawn of Qumran*.

3. Sanders, *Torah and Canon* (1st ed.), ix–xx; Sanders, "Adaptable for Life"; Sanders, "The Canonical Process."

4. Semler, *Abhandlung*.

5. Ulrich, "The Notion and Definition of Canon."

This soon brought focus on the recitals one frequently finds in Torah, Prophets, Psalms, and some of the other Writings: the story of the Exodus–Wanderings–Entrance of the escaped Hebrew slaves from Egypt, "the people come out of Egypt," who settled in Canaan. Why is that sequence of events so often repeated, as many biblical passages indicate? The focus of study then shifted for some of us in the field from canon as the final stage of the formation of the Bible to why such a story as that was repeated in the first place, well before anything like a complete canon or Bible came into being. What value was derived from repeating this sequence? One has generally assumed it was because the particular sequence of events was the basis of the national epic, and that is undoubtedly right. But it seemed important enough a question to seek an answer. Years of experience reading and teaching the Bible offered a beginning point.[6]

When one culls out of the biblical text all the passages in which the recital of the Exodus–Wanderings–Entrance story appears, a pattern emerges: careful review of all the fuller passages that included reference to that basic story showed that it had become a touchstone of authority, a kind of protocanon or early canon (as function) for numerous speakers and writers—early and late—in the Bible. Even references to "plagues" in later literature (cf. Zech 14:15, 18) appear to have been echoes of the plagues God had brought on Egypt in the exodus. To refer to that event meant the author wanted to ring in the changes of epic authority to support whatever argument s/he was making. It appears in various forms in the preexilic prophets at the point where reference to the authority of Israel's defining story was made to support a point the prophet wanted to stress about the potential disaster looming in the rise of the Iron-Age Mesopotamian powers, and then in the early postexilic prophets to make the claim that the return was a repeat of the exodus (*typos* and *antitypos*). It appears in Psalms where the basic epic story braces a summary history of old Israel. It appears in postexilic literature with the addition of exilic and postexilic events to affirm continuity of the new Judaism with old

6. Sanders, *Torah and Canon* (2nd ed.), 95–203.

Israel and Judah. It forms the content of the last chapters of Sirach (Ecclesiasticus), and it appears in the long recital by Stephen before the high priest and the council members of the Synagogue of the Freedmen in Jerusalem to claim that the God who had worked through the earlier events had also worked in and through Jesus Christ (Acts 7).

The recital was thus clearly elastic. The addition of earlier patriarchal and Genesis traditions were among the first expansions, and the addition of the exile and return were added in due course, with Luke understanding that it was the very basis of self-understanding of the first Christians in Stephen's defense before the Synagogue council. The Christian First Testament in Catholic and various Orthodox churches, similar to and yet quite different in number and order of books from the Tanakh, exploited the elasticity of the First Testament recitals—by adding to the "historical" or third section all the books that would indicate that God's work in Israel's history stretched down to the Maccabean Period so that the Gospels and Acts could be appended to it, as Stephen's speech clearly indicates.

Narrative Recitals and Exodus Allusions[7]

The following is an overview of the appearances of the recital in the Bible:

I. Recitals

Lev 23:43—Exodus–Wanderings as authority for Festival of Succot

Num 20:14–16—Exodus–Wanderings as authority of people wishing to transverse Edom

---

7. Thanks to my student David Kitsch for his assistance in compiling this list.

Deut 4:33–38—Exodus–Wanderings as authority for keeping laws

Deut 6:21–23—Exodus–Entrance as authority for the laws

Deut 8:14–16—Exodus–Wanderings as warning not to forget to obey God's laws

Deut 11:2–7—Exodus–Wanderings as authority for laws

Deut 26:5–9—Genesis–Exodus–Wanderings–Entrance as liturgy of thanksgiving

Deut 29:2–7—Exodus–Wanderings as authority for laws

Josh 24:2–13—Genesis (Patriarchs & Descent)–Exodus–Wanderings–Entrance as reason to worship Yahweh after conquest

Judg 2:1–2—Exodus–Entrance as authority for God to judge his own people

Judg 6:8–10—Exodus–Wanderings–Entrance as authority for prophet's words

1 Sam 10:18—Exodus–Wanderings by Samuel as authority for opposing monarchy

1 Sam 12:8—Genesis–Exodus–Entrance as authority for making Saul king

Neh 9:6–31—Creation–Patriarchs–Exodus–Wanderings–Entrance–Exile–Restoration in a public confession of sin on the rise of anti-Semitism in fifth-century Persian Empire

Ps 78:8–12—Jacob's Descent–Exodus–Wanderings–Entrance–Exile–Restoration–David on the sins of Northern Israel and divine favor of Judah

Ps 81:10—Yahweh, identified as the LORD of the exodus, laments people's sins

Ps 105:7–45—Patriarchs–Descent–Exodus–Entrance in hymn of thanksgiving

Ps 106:7–46—Exodus–Wanderings–Entrance–Exile in hymn of thanksgiving and plea for return from exile

Ps 135:8–12—Exodus–Entrance in hymn of praise

Ps 136:4–22—Creation–Exodus–Entrance in hymn of thanksgiving

Jer 2:6–7—Exodus–Wanderings–Entrance as authority for indictment of sins

Jer 7:21–28—Exodus–Wanderings as authoritative period for God's will and laws

Jer 11:4–5—Exodus–Wanderings as authoritative period for God's will and laws

Jer 23:7–8—Exodus–Wanderings–Entrance as typology for return

Jer 32:20–23—Creation–Exodus–Entrance as authority for prophetic indictments of Israel

Hos 2:14–15—Exodus–Wanderings as model for how Israel should respond to new exodus

Hos 8:13 & 9:6—threat to return to Egypt

Hos 9:10—Wanderings: authority for the relation of Yahweh to Israel

Hos 11:1—Egypt, the basic call of Israel as Yahweh's son out of Egypt

Hos 11:9 & 12:4—Yahweh Israel's LORD and savior since Egypt

Hos 12:13—Egypt whence LORD brought Israel up by a prophet

Amos 2:9–10—Entrance–Exodus to contrast Yahweh's deeds with Israel's

Amos 3:1–2—Exodus–Wanderings to affirm election as authority for judgments

Amos 9:7—Exodus–Wanderings compared to migrations of other nations led by Yahweh

Mic 6:4–5—Exodus–Wanderings–Balaam's oracles–Entrance as basis of ethics for Israel

Acts 7:2–50—Genesis–Exodus–Wanderings–David/Solomon as authority for indicting those who reject messianic claims for Jesus

Jdt 5:6–19—Patriarchs–Exodus–Entrance–Exile–Return— recital by Achio the Ammonite to Holophernes, the Aassyrian commander to suggest Israel's sins as their Achilles' heel

2 Esd 3:4–27—Adam–Flood–Patriarchs–Exodus–Sinai–Entrance–David–Exile as authority for citing sinful heart of Israel

2 Esd 14:3–4—Exodus–Wanderings–Sinai: authority for Moses analogous to Ezra

Sirach 44–50, et al., among the longer recitals in Anglican, Lutheran, Catholic, and Orthodox canons

II. Reference to Exodus only

Lev 11:45—Exodus as authority for *kashrut* laws

Lev 19.34—Exodus as authority for treatment of aliens in the Land

Lev 19:36—Exodus as authority for laws of weights and measures

Lev 22:33—Exodus as authority for laws in general

Lev 25:38—Exodus for authority of Jubilee law against interest loans

Lev 25:42—Exodus as authority of Jubilee law of release of Hebrew slaves

Lev 25:55—Exodus as authority of Jubilee law of redemption of Hebrew indebted to alien

Lev 26:13—Exodus as authority for divine blessings and curses

Lev 26:45—Exodus as authority for understanding divine judgments and land lying fallow

Num 15:41—Exodus as authority for tassels

Num 23:22 & 24:8—Exodus as authority for Israel's continuing strength

Deut 1:30—Exodus as authority for belief in God as Holy Warrior

Deut 4:20—Exodus as authority for First Commandment

Deut 5:6—Exodus as authority for First Commandment (and for Decalogue?)

Deut 5:15—Exodus as authority for Sabbath law

Deut 6:12—Exodus as authority for remembering indebtedness to Yahweh

Deut 7:7-8, 18-19—Exodus as authority for laws

Deut 9:26-29—plea by Moses that God remember the exodus and its purpose

Deut 10:19—Exodus as the authority for loving the sojourner

Deut 13:5—law against false prophets who cause people to forget exodus

Deut 13:10—law against family who cause people to forget exodus

Deut 15:15—Exodus as authority for Jubilee release of slaves

Deut 16:1—Exodus as reason to keep the Passover

Deut 20:1—Yahweh holy warrior same as God of exodus

Deut 24:17-18—Exodus as the authority for justice due the dispossessed

Deut 24:22—Exodus as the model for leaving produce in field for others

Deut 29:25—Exodus as authority of Yahweh to judge his own people

Deut 34:11–12—Moses unique as leader of the exodus

Judg 2:12—Exodus as authority for God to judge his own people

1 Sam 8:8—Exodus as authority for God to judge people for desiring a king

1 Sam 12:6—Exodus as identity of Yahweh

2 Sam 7:5–16 (// 1 Kgs 8:16–21)—Yahweh itinerant or tutelary deity since Exodus

1 Kgs 8:9—Exodus as authority for covenant and placing ark in Solomon's temple

1 Kgs 8:9—ark with 2 tablets since exodus

1 Kgs 8:51–53—Israel Yahweh's people since exodus

1 Kgs 9:9—Exodus as authority for Yahweh to judge his own people

1 Kgs 12:28—Jeroboam claims golden calves brought the people from Egypt

2 Kgs 17:7—Exodus as authority for God to judge Israel using Assyria

2 Kgs 17:36—Exodus as authority for God to judge his own people

1 Chr 17:21–22—Exodus as authority for uniqueness of Israel

2 Chr 6:5 = 1 Kgs 8:15–16

2 Chr 7:12–22—Exodus as authority for God to judge his own people

Isa 10:26—Exodus as authority for prediction that Assyria will be like Egypt

Jer 11:7 —Exodus as authority for command to obey God's voice

Jer 16:14–15—Exodus the model for the new exodus (see Jer 31:31–33)

Jer 23:7–8—Exodus as the model for the new exodus (see above)

Jer 34:13—Exodus as authority for Jubilee release of Hebrew slaves

Ezek 20:10—Exodus–Wanderings as authority for ordinances

Mic 7:15—Exodus as model for divine marvels to come

2 Esd 1:7—Exodus as authority for indictments of his own people

Bar 1:19–20—Israel sinful since the exodus

Jude 5—Exodus as authority for judging God's own people

The recital is also included in common Christian liturgy—for instance, the Eucharistic Prayer that includes echoes of Genesis 1–25, Exodus, and the Prophets, then moves directly to the Christ events. One should note too that the order of books in the First Testament, in contrast to the Hebrew Bible order, gathers all the so-called historical books in a supposed chronological order in order for the faithful to see that God's work then continued on into the events of the New Testament, with the Prophetic Corpus arranged last supposedly foretelling those events.

The pattern is clear that when a speaker or writer needed to bolster an argument about what God was doing in and for Israel in their time, a reference to the defining events of Israel's origins was made in order to lend authority to the argument. It was recited to authorize an event such as the anointing of Saul (1 Sam 12:8) or other positive uses. What happened back then was indicative, it was argued, of what was happening in their time. Amos in his stunning sermon at the royal sanctuary in Bethel in the northern kingdom in the middle of the eighth century BCE made a shocking comparison between the justice God had done for the poor and dispossessed slaves in the exodus event and the injustice its heirs were doing to the poor and dispossessed in their own country under Jeroboam II (Amos 2:9–10). When Israel was poor and powerless in Egypt, God sent Moses and effected the

The Monotheizing Process

Exodus–Wanderings–Entrance event that delivered the Hebrews from Egypt and gave them a place to live. But when Israel came into power of its own and had its own land, it did not do for its poor what God had done for them in Egypt but rather imitated what Pharaoh had done to the Hebrew slaves back then.

It is thus impelling that reference to the formative events of Israel's beginnings constituted a kind of authority sought in making the reference. It is apparently inescapable that for many writings that ended up in the Bible, the Exodus–Wanderings–Entrance story had a kind of authority that was available to be drawn from when indicated.

Two of the earliest such clear references appear in 1 Samuel 10–12. In 10:18, Samuel is reported to have used the reference to oppose kingship whereas in 12:6–8 he uses the same reference to support it. In 12:6, reference is made to the exodus event in order to provide identity for Yahweh, who, Samuel dared claim (in early Greek translations following 12:5), was witness to the event taking place. But then, lo and behold, in 12:8 Samuel is described as addressing the people assembled in Gilgal to make Saul king; he then provides readers with a kind of liturgical chant that ostensibly served as appeal to authority for what was going to take place, namely the anointing of Saul as the first king of Israel, the northern tribes.

Our purpose here is not to discuss the history of the formation of the text of 1 Samuel, but to discern what the text as it comes down to us indicates about the citation in it of the familiar story the recitals recount. No matter the explanation for the contradictions, they serve to show that if there were kings in ancient Israel, Yahweh of necessity sanctioned the monarchy; but if the monarchy finally failed, that too was ordained by Yahweh. In any case, the recital in 1 Sam 12:8 Samuel begins with reference to the tradition of Jacob's descent to Egypt, the account of which the end of the Joseph story in Genesis provides. First Samuel then reflects on the oppression of the Hebrew people in Egypt and Yahweh's sending Moses and Aaron to effect their deliverance in the Exodus and Entrance "to dwell in this place"—all in one verse! This is the shortest of the recitals in the Bible of the three-point history, with its elasticity evident already in the inclusion of terse reference to Jacob's descent into Egypt in Genesis. There are more cursive references to the Exodus alone, which indicate claim to authority. But those, as may be seen in the above lists, serve largely as identity for the Yahweh mentioned in each text, as in 1 Sam 12:6. The story begins by indicating that Yahweh was present for the anointing about to take place. But it is in 1 Sam 12:8 that the story, of what Yahweh had done in the Genesis–Exodus–Joshua accounts, appears as a kind of liturgical recital invoked as authorization of the coronation.

The fact that the Deuteronomic historian evidently had no problem in making reference to the same founding events to oppose kingship and then shortly thereafter to support it should not be surprising. Ancient historians were considerably less disturbed by apparent contradictions of the sort when they needed to use the vehicle of authority an older tradition afforded; they daren't change too much the vehicle they wanted to ride to make their points, or they'd lose the authority they sought.[8]

In the case of the contradictions in 1 Samuel 8–12 between Samuel's promonarchical and antimonarchical positions the tension served well the monotheizing process that the Bible describes: if there was indeed a monarchy, and historically there was, according to the biblical text, then Yahweh must have wanted it; but if the monarchy eventually failed, as indeed it did, then that too must have been the will of Yahweh. Such passages in the Bible match others, such as the hardening of the heart of Pharaoh in Exodus and the hardening of the hearts of the people by the preaching of the prophet Isaiah in Isa 6:9–10, to illustrate the monotheizing process that the Bible as a whole describes.

A text viewed by most as an important juncture in the Deuteronomic argument, which offers the founding story as a liturgical recital claiming authority for the event in which it is recited is Deut 26:5–9. The passage appears at the close of the listing of laws given on Mount Horeb in Deuteronomy 12–25 and just before the listing of curses for disobedience and blessings for obedience

8. Akenson, *Surpassing Wonder*, 40.

in Deuteronomy 27–28, that conclude the basic statement of the covenant that the book of Deuteronomy advances. Deuteronomy 29–31 then provide a summary of the Deuteronomic view of the covenant, and chapter 32 a poetic recap of it, while chapter 33 records Moses's blessings on the tribes about to cross the Jordan, and chapter 34 his death. Deuteronomy 26 occurs, in other words, at the conclusion of the "second giving" of the law just before the hortatory section and narrative closing of the book. Its importance cannot be overstated despite efforts to belittle it.[9]

Chapter 26 begins with the stirring words, "When you come into the land . . ." Those words, in the mouth of Moses, who would not accompany them, would have had special meaning for Israel on numerous occasions when recited in later history, especially at the return at the end of the exile. The words introduce a final piece of Deuteronomic legislation, a liturgy of thanksgiving for God's fulfilling the promise of God to Abram in Genesis 12 of a place to live. Instruction is given on what to do to observe the thanksgiving service: the adherent is to take a basket of fruit produced after settlement in the land to the place God will designate, offer it on the altar there, and say to the priest in charge the following recital: "A wandering (perishing?) Aramaean was my father (Jacob) when he descended to Egypt to live there and eventually prosper after which a Pharaoh arose who afflicted them with hard bondage. We (*sic*) cried to Yahweh who heard our cry, saw our sufferings, toil, and oppression and brought us out of Egypt with wondrous effect and brought into this land flowing with milk and honey" (Deut 26:5–9). Note the implied identity of the later generations reciting the epic story, a point indicating its authority for later times. Here the story is succinctly told with events summarized that are fully developed in Genesis, Exodus, and Joshua.

But note, that like the shorter recital in 1 Sam 12:8, it says nothing about the wanderings in the desert. In fact, one astounding observation that needs to be made is that none of the recitals (note the lists above) says anything about a stop at Sinai (or Horeb). This raises the question of when the Exodus story was wed to the

---

9. Barr, *The Concept of Biblical Theology*, 49.

Sinai/Horeb (the giving-of-the-law) events. The merger apparently happened late in the exile or in Early Judaism (Neh 9:6–31).[10] As one moves down through the above list, it is clear that until the exile the recitals did not include a stop at Sinai or any suggestion of the revealing of a set of laws during the recital period, all of which, in the final form of the narrative text, are grouped in the Sinai Pericope (Exodus 19 to Numbers 10) and in the book of Deuteronomy at Horeb (Deuteronomy 12–26) on the east bank of the Jordan River.

One would expect laws to appear at least as royal decrees or judgments (the source of most laws in the ancient Near East) in the books of Samuel or Kings, but no book after the Torah includes any such laws; they were all gathered from various sources and grouped as coming from the recital period, either at Sinai or at Horeb, and that would have occurred in the Early Jewish Period under the leadership of the continuing Deuteronomistic school and of the priestly leadership that took control of surviving Judaism in the early postexilic or Persian period.

Another adjustment made to meet historical need also took place in the Early Persian or Jewish period: the omission of the book of Joshua from the Torah's recital narrative. This undoubtedly happened at the beginnings of Early Judaism in the early Persian Period and probably in Babylonia where Ezra gained the title of Scribe and edited the Torah in its (close-to) final form. Ezra then brought it with him from Babylonia to Jerusalem and read it from a dais built in the Water Gate area of Jerusalem from dawn 'til noon, with Levites translating his readings into Aramaic, the language of the local population by then (Nehemiah 8).[11] The Deuteronomic (-istic) school, which continued into earliest post-Exilic times editing the books of Samuel and Kings, had already determined that Moses was the hero of the Exodus and Wanderings up to the east bank of the Jordan so that it became easy to cut the story off at his death rather than include the fulfillment book of Joshua, which records differing accounts of the settlement

10. Noth, *History of Israel*.

11. Sanders, *Torah and Canon* (2nd ed.), 95–103.

in the Land, the Entrance part of the early recitals lacking in the final Torah. Why was the Entrance, so vital and constant a part of the recitals, omitted from the final form of the recital, the Torah (Genesis to Deuteronomy)?

Because the Torah was in fact edited in Babylonia where the largest Jewish community resided from the sixth century BCE until the sixth century CE (when the official Jewish Talmud, the *Bavli*, was edited there) so that it would have been difficult at best to have the first settlement in Canaan as the climax of Torah. That ended in disaster as is clear in the Deuteronomic history through to the end of 2 Kings, and, more important, served as explanation for why God had used Assyria and Babylonia to effect it. Furthermore, Ezra's sponsors and followers in Babylon clearly did not want to hear that one would have to live down there in that desolate place to be a real Jew. They undoubtedly persuaded Ezra to make Moses's noble death on Mount Pisgah's lofty heights in Transjordan the climax of their basic identifying narrative—the Torah. They were quite willing to sponsor the resettlement, even the rebuilding of Jerusalem (as recorded in Ezra/Nehemiah), but not to leave their newfound lives in Babylonia after the Persian liberation there from the Neo-Babylonian Empire. In a similar way modern, loyal Jews scattered in Europe and the Americas sponsor the modern State of Israel but have no intention of moving there. Those who had once been in Babylonian prison camps under the Babylonians, or the next generations, now found liberated life there much to their liking. Archaeology has shown that the Return to the Land anthemed in the exilic Isaiah's prophecies (Isaiah 40–55) was actually quite underwhelming. While remaining in Diaspora many undoubtedly supported the resettlement in the Land but would not themselves return. The Diaspora, which began with the Babylonian exile, for the majority of Judaism has persisted through to modern times.

The function of these early recitals indicates that canon was not meant at first to be understood as "the Word of God." A community recited its canon, at whatever stage in its development, to *affirm* the ways of God with humans and to discern what God was doing in their day. With the steady though bumpy process in the biblical text to affirm the oneness of God over against various sorts of polytheism ever present in the biblical text, the basic meaning of canon took shape. In effect, a canon is in large part a paradigm for learning to conjugate the verbs and decline the nouns of the monotheizing process.

Canon and the Monotheizing Process

Along with the gradual development of a protocanon of recitals of God's involvement with Israel there also developed the concept of there being but One God of All. Monotheism, like canons, did not start full-blown by the decree of a king or central government. It developed out of the necessity early on to unify the ancient tribes that made up the early Israelite coalition of groups that in various ways replaced the Canaanites in the Palestinian area. Joshua 24 represents a Deuteronomistic effort to see Yahweh as One Yahweh following the Josianic Reformation of the late seventh century and the discovery of a Torah scroll in the temple under restoration (2 Kings 22–23). Deuteronomy 6:4, the *Shema'*, is at the center of every Jewish worship service down to today: "Hear, O Israel, Yahweh our God is one Yahweh."

The antecedents to the Deuteronomic affirmation of one God, Yahweh, for all the remaining tribes in the seventh century cannot be known with certainty. The predecessors of the one God Yahweh cannot be known because it is not exactly clear how worshipers within earlier traditions perceived the various names of their gods. Genesis 4:26 clearly states that "folk began to call upon the name of Yahweh" in the time of Seth and his son, Enosh. But it is generally agreed that because Gen 4:26 directly contradicts the statement in Exod 6:3 that none of the patriarchs knew a god by the name Yahweh, therefore Gen 4:26 was probably a later editorial effort to read Yahwism back into the period after the expulsion from Eden. The Exodus passage claims, on the contrary, that it was Moses who first was told to call God Yahweh, and that the patriarchs called God by various names, including: the Shield (*magen*) of Abraham (Gen 14:20), the Fear (*pachad*) of Isaac (Gen 31:42), and the Mighty

One (*'avir*) of Jacob (Gen 49:14). On the other hand, a number of other names for God (also known as names for other Canaanite or Northwest Semitic deities) were used, such as *El, El Shaddai,* and *El Elyon.*[12] Remarkably the Bible rarely tries to harmonize such contradictory views but keeps some tribal views of God in the monotheizing process, thus heralding the eventual biblical view of the One God of All as having the traits of the earlier deities—being both familiarly immanent (Genesis 2), and ineffably transcendent (Genesis 1). Biblically, God has the traits of creator and redeemer, of being both far off and near, as Jeremiah declaimed (Jer 23:23). The rabbis later claimed that the One God had seventy different names—a clear move in the monotheizing process.

Jeremiah ministered in the southern kingdom of Judah, benefitting from the messages of the prophets who had preached during the second half of the previous century, when the Assyrians destroyed the northern kingdom of Israel and conquered Judah, laying siege to Jerusalem but stopping short of actually taking it. Jeremiah's message marked a crucial turning in the monotheizing process, making it clear that God was not just Yahweh of old but the One God of all creation. In his debate with Hananiah (Jeremiah 28), who preached that Yahweh would not let Jerusalem be captured by the Babylonians, Jeremiah proclaimed Judah's end at Babylonian hands; he preached that Babylon's king, Nebudchad-nezzar, was a servant of God. In his message, Jeremiah still used the name Yahweh and thus witnessed to the monotheizing process in dramatic fashion by claiming that Yahweh, Judah's name for God, was the God of the Babylonians as well as of Judah. Jeremiah learned well from Amos, Hosea, Micah, and Isaiah: God was no longer just a tribal god but the God of both parties of a conflict.[13] And yet the One God of All was still considered close to the people, retaining the traits of the earlier local deities. The combination of transcendence and immanence has been retained by both Judaism and Christianity, with the concept of *Shekinah* (indwelling spirit

12. Rose, "Names of God"; Albertz, *A History of Israelite Religion,* vol. 1; and Smith, *The Origins of Biblical Monotheism.*

13. Sanders, "Hermeneutics of True and False Prophecy."

of God for Jews) and Holy Spirit (for Christians) continuing to be integral parts of both understandings down to today.

3

The Prophets
and the Monotheizing Process

Amos and the Prophet

The prophet Amos's sermons and speeches may serve as examples of the messages of the other pre-Exilic judgmental prophets. Amos, the first historically of those in the Prophetic Corpus, addressed the leaders of northern Israel, who in the middle of the eighth century BCE had become proud of their successes under Jeroboam II and felt that Yahweh surely would be pleased with them and reward them, and might even appear on "The Day of the Lord" to honor their efforts on God's behalf (Amos 5:18–20). Amos's sermon, recorded in Amos 1:3—3:2, comes alive in brilliant relief against a backdrop of national pride being celebrated on a high holy day such as the annual New Year ceremonies, when Yahweh might be expected to make a congratulatory appearance, a *parousia*, so to speak.

But Amos would also have known that the Assyrian Empire to the northeast was on the move and expanding by harsh military means. News spread more rapidly in antiquity than moderns perhaps think it did. Caravans and various travelers steadily crossing through the region from Mesopotamia to Egypt and Europe to Asia would have carried news relatively fast and reached even

Tekoa, where Amos lived. To object that Tekoa was remote out in the Judaean desert is beside the point; that would have meant a few days' delay at most. Market day each week would have been the vehicle for widespread dissemination of news through the region. Even today locals in the Near East depend on news spread by (scheduled) service-taxi travelers more than on the news reported on television and radio; the latter are usually state-run and nowhere near as trustworthy in their minds as news spread by travelers like themselves. It is one of the major functions of service travel, during which the different sojourners in a long-distance taxi share and pool what they know and then spread it upon arrival, just as travelers in ancient caravans would have done. Amos in particular would have benefitted from the circle of Wisdom thinkers known at Tekoa (cf. 2 Sam 14:1–24), who would have depended on their perspective to interpret the news. Wisdom thinking undoubtedly influenced Amos's information and thought patterns as can be seen in his style of speech[1] and in how he subverted reference to the national epic in his speeches.

Amos referred to Israel's precious traditions about the Exodus, Wanderings, and Entrance into the Land (2:9–12) not to support the leaders' pride but to challenge it by saying that even given these venerable traditions, they were treating the poor in the land the way Pharaoh had treated them when they were poor and in bondage in Egypt. Instead of pursuing the Way of Yahweh now that they had the opportunity to do so, in mistreating the poor in Israel, they were instead following the way of Pharaoh (Amos 2:6–12). Why had they done so? Amos made it clear that it was mainly because of idolatry, the sin of loving God's creation or God's gifts (in any form) more than God, the Giver of all gifts. That is the basic meaning of idolatry, exemplified by but not limited to making statues and figurines of creation's resources to worship,

---

1. Terrien, "Amos and Wisdom." McLaughlin, "Is Amos (Still) among the Wise?" has reviewed the literature following Terrien's article. None of the literature since Terrien makes the case here pursued. McLaughlin concludes his review by arguing against any wisdom influence in Amos but does not consider wisdom's influence on the hermeneutic by which Amos reread (*en relecture*) the national epic.

thus loving God's gifts and forgetting that God gave them all that they had: land, prosperity, everything—even the materials used to make idols—and with false pride calling themselves exceptional because of those gifts. The year was 750 BCE when Israel was able to prosper because the power of Egypt, the longtime overlord of Palestine, was waning at the moment, and Israel could thus assert itself. But Amos pointed out that God could raise a foreign power to overwhelm them and subjugate Israel, and was doing so in the rise of the neo-Assyrian Empire under Sargon II. The leaders believed that Yahweh was strong enough to protect his people against foreign gods, whereas Amos believed that Yahweh was strong and big enough to judge and punish his own people when they committed wrong.

The first point on the hermeneutical triangle, introduced above on p. 2, is the text and all that it entails. As part of their work of interpretation, students should try to find out as much as possible about Israel's or Judah's social and political context (the second point of the triangle) that the tradent was addressing. Only in this way can the references and points scored in the passage be clearly discerned and connected. Paul's letters in the New Testament come alive when their intended audience and their concerns are correctly discerned. Noting again the sermon the prophet Amos preached at the royal sanctuary in Bethel in northern Israel, it is mandatory to be aware of the problems he was addressing. The first verse of the book of Amos gives the date of ca. 750 BCE as the time of Amos's ministry. When the serious student looks at the situation in northern Israel at that time, it is clear that the little kingdom under Jeroboam II was prospering because Egypt's power was waning. Israel's borders had expanded, and its expeditionary forces had scored some victories, notably one in Gilead across the Jordan (Amos 6:13). The leaders apparently took great pride in their prowess, and it was this that Amos railed against as much as anything else, including their treating the poor in their own land the way Pharaoh had treated them in Egypt. Israel's leaders felt that Yahweh must surely be proud of them for expanding to borders almost as extensive in the north as they had been in Solomon's day. They were apparently expecting God to honor them for their deeds "on God's behalf." They were gathering in the sanctuary at Bethel probably to celebrate the annual New Year's festival when the "Day of the LORD" would manifest itself—to their honor and benefit, of course.

It was into that situation of national pride that Amos declaimed his proclamation of indictments and sentences against their pride and misguided claims of exceptionalism. They felt they were different from all others, and Amos at the end of his sermon exclaims that while they are right about being the only family on earth that Yahweh knew, it was because they woefully misunderstood election that God was going to punish them (Amos 3:1–2). At one point Amos even declared that while Israelites were certainly right to claim that God had led them in their escape from Egypt's bondage, they should be aware that God had also led the Philistines in their migration from Caphtor and the Syrians from Kir (Amos 9:7). He even in the same verse claims that Israel is in the mind of God no more than Ethiopia. Amos's message was such a shock to exceptionalist thinking that he was thrown out of town and kingdom for preaching such negative things (Amos 7:12–13).

It is only in studying Amos in the social and political context in which his sermon was delivered that students see the power of it—and can make the appropriate analogy for reading it today—so that one can ask, is there a people today who claim special exceptionalism because of their belief in being chosen and blessed by God? Where and when does such belief become pride and cause blindness to what is being done to the poor and the dispossessed today?

One might well ask why such sermons and oracles as Amos's, rejected when first heard, were recalled and recited in Babylonian prison camps enough to get onto a kind of tenure track toward a canon! The reason is clear. Without persuasive explanations of why old Israel and Judah were destroyed, it would have been impossible to build the new Judaism on the promises and traditions the Torah heralds, which had given them birth in the first place. That is, in fact, the major function of the prophetic corpus in the Tanakh—to explain the failure. None of Israel's neighbors, also conquered by Assyria and Babylonia, survived the disaster, but Israel did sur- vive, as the new Israel (called Judaism), which was born out of the ashes of the First Temple. The prophetic literature that explained the disaster also provided means of hope beyond the disaster by insisting that no horror or disaster is beyond the One God's ability to redeem.[2] These two functions of the Prophetic Corpus prepared the way for the foundation of Early Judaism, but neither would have been sufficient without the belief that the God of Judah and Israel was indeed the One God of All who could oversee the fail- ure of the first Israel in order to prepare for the second—Judaism. Today we should understand that God was never actually the God of Judah and Israel, or indeed the God of the Bible, but that the One true God of All was working in and through ancient Israel's culture-bound Yahweh, and since then through the peculiar ideas about God in the major religions, patiently hoping we very limited humans may come to worship the One God of All.

Discerning the hermeneutics (the third point in the triangle) by which the prophet or tradent reread the old traditions is as im- portant as discerning the composition of the text studied (the first point) and the sociopolitical situation it addressed (the second point). It means that students should try as carefully as possible to discern the hermeneutic by which the tradent of a passage caused older references and traditions to be relevant to the ancient situa- tion addressed. The book of Amos continues to be illustrative. One can see in what Amos preached at Bethel in northern Israel, and in the Amos book generally, that his references to earlier traditions, such as the Exodus–Wanderings–Entrance recital, were made in order to contrast what God had done for ancient Israelites when they were poor and dispossessed in Egypt to what Israelites of Amos's day were doing to the poor in the land.

Amos castigates the countries all around Israel for having maltreated their neighbors, but at the climax of the sermon, in a dramatically rhetorical move, he accuses Israel of maltreating their own people, the powerless in their own land (Amos 1:3—2:12).

2. Sanders, *Torah and Canon* (2nd ed.), 54–88.

How could Amos refer to the precious national traditions in the way that he did when they were normally recited to assert Israel's special identity as God's elect? In the same manner that some today are incensed when America's or modern Israel's exceptionalism is questioned, so back then were the good people of Israel outraged at Amos for suggesting that God was not on their side or proud of them for expanding Israel's borders and influence in the area. But Amos, on the contrary, read the same national traditions about the Exodus and settlement in Canaan to express the belief that Yahweh chose them not for favor but to be exceptionally just in their treatment of the poor and powerless in their own land, as God had been exceptionally just in liberating the slaves from bondage in Egypt.

Amos's expanding view of Yahweh determined how he read and applied tradition to eighth-century-BCE northern Israel. Polytheism would have understood Yahweh as a national deity whose divine self-interest was to sponsor and support the people or nation under his aegis. But when Wisdom thinking began to expand the concept of Yahweh to international dimensions, one's review and rereading (*relecture*) of those traditions rendered a quite different message.

In Amos 3:1–2 Amos apparently responded to an interlocutor, who had objected to Amos's sermon by insisting that God had chosen Israel out of all the families of the earth. Amos agrees with his interlocutor but adds that God expects Israel to act like a chosen people. Amos's call is a resounding blow against the common views of national exceptionalism. Amos then adds that God will punish Israel. One can be sure that those who heard the interchange would have been furious at Amos's idea that God would fail to act toward his chosen people as they expected God to do. Conventional thought in Amos's day included an argument typical of polytheism: a people's god would favor its own.

Amos uses the very same national recital tradition (which typically buttressed exceptionalism) as authority for his message of divine indictment against Israel for failing to act the way they should have. Amos goes even further by outrageously suggesting that Israel's migration from Egypt to Canaan was but one such migration Yahweh had overseen! "Are you not like the Ethiopians to me? Did I not bring Israel up from Egypt, the Philistines from Caphtor and the Syrians from Kir?" (9:7). Amos in effect says that Israel's claiming exceptionalism and citing the gospel story of redemption from slavery in Egypt makes their migration directly comparable to other such migrations that God had also guided. Such an idea would have been anathema to the priests and officials who heard Amos's sermon. Why? Because prevenient grace and election slip very easily into ideas of immunity and impunity; prevenient grace (or forgiveness of sins in advance of their being committed) coupled with the idea of being chosen slip into the worst kinds of imperial ideas of might making right, when those who claim it wield the power. Modern readers in the West would do well in the exchange to identify not with Amos but with the religious leaders of ancient Israel in order to feel how Amos's statements infuriated the comparable leaders back then. This is called dynamic analogy. Again, knowing the situations in which the biblical passage was originally heard and the hermeneutic by which it was applied are key to its first meanings, including the meanings that eventually gained the Amos book entry into the Early Jewish canon.

The meaning that Amos's message held for those in exile later emerged in their efforts to build the nascent Judaism. It was their task to build Judaism out of the ashes of the old kingdoms of Israel and Judah. Thus Amos and the other prophets, reviled in their time, became during the exile extremely important for explaining how and why ancient Israel and Judah were destroyed, and how God through the adversity was forging a new Israel to arise out of the debris of the old. If Amos and other prophets did not offer such an explanation, there would have been no basis for claiming that God's promises to the patriarchs of progeny and land (Gen 12:1–7) were still valid in building the new Israel, Early Judaism.

The task of the exiles was to construct Judaism based on an understanding of the monotheizing process that the prophets had expounded in their time. For modern Western readers to agree with Amos and to look down on those he castigates is a false reading of the text and misses the point altogether. Modern readers should identify with those to whom the message of the prophets, or Jesus, spoke in order to discern the impact of the message—then and now. Their message can still be as disturbing today to both religious and secular folk as it was back then—especially to those who subscribe to national exceptionalism or even to the uniqueness of modern Islam, Judaism, or Christianity for understanding the work of God in the world today.

The Prophets and Wisdom

But where did Amos get such ideas? How did he arrive at the idea of Yahweh's being the God of Ethiopians, Philistines, and Syrians (Amos 9:7)—indeed of Israel's neighboring peoples (1:3—2:5)—as well as of Israel? This meant that Yahweh was in Amos's mind no longer the God of Israel only but also the God of neighbors near and far (cf. Jer 23:23). His ideas deeply offended the leaders and others who heard him (7:10-13), and there is no evidence of such ideas having been so starkly expressed before Amos.

The traditions that the prophets cited as the authority for their messages included early nascent ideas of God's being the God also of other peoples, as when the Exodus traditions say (fourteen times) that God "hardened the heart of Pharaoh." The very idea that God would sympathize with the Egyptian pharaoh and his responsibility for the economy of the nation he ruled upheld by the cheap slave labor the Hebrews in Egypt provided—basically the position of the deeply Christian Confederacy in the American Civil War—is not one we now want to hear about any more than the leaders in ancient Israel wanted to hear Amos's ideas about God's being the God also of others: particularly when those others included some of Israel's worst enemies like the Philistines and the Syrians.[3] What kind of a God is that? The answer to that question is the one the Bible gives in its overall monotheizing message: God

3. Sanders, "The Betrayal."

is not just Yahweh, but the One God of All—despite the fact that many early traditions of the Bible seem to cast Yahweh as Israel's tribal, protective deity, the kind of god polytheists understand very well. God was God all along, of course, but people can't hear such affirmations outside their cultural givens, and Israel's cultural given was that Yahweh was their god. In fact, alas, many Jews, Christians, and Muslims are not able openly to continue the monotheizing process because of human cultural givens (tribalism/nationalism and idolatry) today.

Early Judaism after the exile began to forbid the pronunciation of the old preexilic name, Yahweh, substituting the vowels for the title Lord for vowels that possibly had originally been used to pronounce YHWH. The prohibition was so effective that today we make assumptions as to how the consonants YHWH were originally vocalized. It has long been thought that the reason for forbidding the old pronunciation was that God was ineffable and awesome. And that was undoubtedly the case, but the reason for understanding God's becoming so ineffable was that the monotheizing process had reached the point in Early Judaism when God was understood to be not just the old, tribal Yahweh but, on the contrary, the God of All ('elohah ha-kol). The tradition arose then that the One God had seventy names, quite enough to account for the many gods mentioned in Genesis and other early accounts. The Qur'an reflects the same view.

The answer to how Amos could advance the monotheizing process so effectively was undoubtedly to be found in the Wisdom circle of thinkers for which his village, Tekoa, had been known. The wise woman of Tekoa who worked in cahoots with Joab to try to get David to forgive Absalom was one such (2 Samuel 14). In addition, much of the rhetoric Amos used in his sermon and in his oracles would have come from Wisdom modes of expression.[4] What is wisdom in the Bible? The wise man or woman, often called a sage, did not cite national epic recitals or traditions to support the message. On the contrary Wisdom thinkers garnered their advice from observing common human actions and practices unlimited

4. Terrien, "Amos and Wisdom."

by national boundaries, and from observing phenomena of nature that also know no national boundaries (1 Kgs 4:33). Wisdom was often personified as a woman as it is in Proverbs (chapters 8 and 9) and elsewhere, and it is instructive to observe the lives and work of women who were clearly unlimited by national or tribal boundaries. In postbiblical Jewish literature wisdom is often portrayed as a woman, even as a woman who was present with God at creation as God's architect. But back in Amos's time wisdom was often derived, not from the nationalism of politically apt (or inept) males, but from the work of women and the lives of nomads, neither of whom was basically defined or in any way limited by national or tribal narratives or borders. In Wisdom literature, in other words, God was perceived as unlimited by Israel's national boundaries or traditions. Amos, genius that he was even as a rural shepherd and dresser of sycamore trees, figured it out for himself: that if the rising and threatening Assyrian Empire to the northeast did indeed come down "like a wolf on the fold," limiting Yahweh to Israel's primal interests, as the national epic had been recited to that point, that would mean the end of Yahweh, because nothing was going to be able to stop the Assyrian onslaught, especially given Egypt's waning power at the time—power on which Israel had long relied.

The prophets who historically follow Amos, those whose sayings survived the canonical process that started in the prisoner-of-war camps in Babylonia two centuries later, were like him in understanding that the concept of a God who would survive disaster could not be limited to the idea of a tribal or national redeemer deity protecting Israel; if so, Yahweh would have disappeared from history with Israel, just like the gods of Israel's many neighbors that suffered the same fate as Israel faced in the Assyrian and then Babylonian invasions. It may to a limited extent have taken contact in those camps with fellow prisoners from other lands who believed in their gods as creator gods for the leaders of the exiles to realize that if Yahwism was to survive the catastrophe that had befallen them, it would have to include creator-god traits. But the seeds of international thinking about the divine had already been sown by the preexilic prophets, influenced by local wisdom thought.

Reflection across three generations of Judaean prisoners during the exile (597–540 BCE) about what the preexilic prophets (hated and rejected back home in the prewar years) had said about Yahweh's being able to appoint and use foreign rulers and conquerors of Israel as instruments of divine judgment of his own people, would have brought these thinkers to see for themselves without such influence that for a remnant of Israel to survive the Iron-Age holocaust, it could no longer hold to an idea of God that was tribal or national. So too Yahweh had to be transformed in their minds into a much broader and larger concept of what God meant.[5] As the Sicilian prince says in Lampedusa's *The Leopard*, "if we want things to stay as they are, things will have to change."[6]

The concept of God could no longer be limited to preexilic, tribal ideas about Yahweh as the God of Israel and Judah but had to be expanded to understand God as being able fully to resignify disaster and suffering not as divine failure but as a radically growing concept of God. Just so, our concept of God today must expand and grow. God is always bigger than we think, and continues to be. Under wisdom influence in Tekoa, for Amos God had to be seen as more than a redeemer from slavery in Egypt (Exodus) or from the Philistine threat of extinction in Canaan (1 Samuel 4—2 Samuel 8); God was also the God of others. This concept of deity easily absorbed the idea of God's being creator of all as well as redeemer of those God had chosen to live lives of Torah—an early concept that ante-dated the completion of the written Torah that Ezra would introduce in Jerusalem in the middle of the fifth century BCE (Nehemiah 8). The basic concepts of Early Judaism had taken shape in the pre-Exilic period—the burden of proof that the books of Chronicles, with their many genealogies reaching back to Adam, sought to advance.

---

5. Sanders and Capetz, "*Credo in Unum Deum.*" See Appendix.
6. Tomasi di Lampedusa, *Il Gattopardo.*

The message of the late eighth-century Isaiah of Jerusalem shows the crucial role hermeneutic plays in reading a text. Isaiah apparently began his ministry the year King Uzziah died, and the best estimate of that date would have been 742 BCE, give or take a couple years. The prophet relates for us his conviction that Yahweh called him to ministry during an experience he had in the Jerusalem temple (Isa 6:1–13). The record we have of his sermons and oracles (embedded in Isaiah 1–39) indicate fairly clearly that early in his ministry Isaiah was convinced of the terms of the Davidic covenant (as recorded in 2 Sam 7:5–16), which assured the kings in the Davidic dynasty that Yahweh would never abrogate the covenant. That conviction led the young Isaiah to assure King Ahaz of Judah in 734 BCE that he need not fear any consequences of the alliance of that time between Syria and northern Israel, which threatened to attack Judah. The sign Isaiah gave the king was that a child born nine or so months after the threat had been issued would be named Emanuel, meaning "God is with us," because by the time the child was delivered, the threat would be past. Isaiah was convinced that all Ahaz had to do was to affirm faith in the Davidic covenant, and all would be well (Isa 7:1–16). And that apparently turned out to be affirmed in that early situation.

But a little over a decade later, in 722 BCE the neo-Assyrian Empire "descended like a wolf on the fold" of the northern kingdom of Israel and conquered it, leaving hardly a trace, obliterating the so-called northern ten tribes. A number of folk, however, from the north escaped and found refuge in Judah to the south to tell of the tragedy and the policy of Assyria to eradicate entirely the identities of those they conquered by deporting large portions of the population to various Assyrian provinces and to admit people from those places into Israel. The northern escapees also apparently shared stories about how Amos, Hosea, and maybe Micah, had warned them that Assyria would do just that, but how they had earlier rejected what those prophets had prophesied. Now, however, they had come to realize the truth of what the prophets had said.

In the light of these events, Isaiah changed his mind, as is recorded in Isa 8:11–15. After the 722 debacle in the north, Isaiah in Jerusalem came to realize that God must be behind what the Assyrians were doing. Isaiah shifted his message dramatically in the light of what Amos and Hosea had preached, and in the light of the demise of the northern kingdom (Isa 28:1–4) he came to see that God was not a guarantor of Judah's continuing unaffected by Assyrian aggression (Isa 7:17–20) but must have chosen Assyria as God's means of judgment against the injustices and idolatries within Judah as well (Isa 10:8–11) in order to purge it of its dross = sins (Isa 1:21–26 *et passim*). In the light of what happened in the years between 742 and 722 Isaiah interpreted his original temple experience as a call from God to preach the way he had in his early ministry. In the famous commission Isaiah received in the temple, Isaiah now understood that God must have earlier ordered him to preach so that the people would not understand the truth of Yahweh's being far more than the national God of Israel and Judah and had chosen Assyria to be the rod of his judgments against his own people. On reflection, Isaiah now understood that in the temple experience what God had commissioned him to do was to preach the old pre-722 message so that the people's heart would be fat, their ears deaf, and their eyes blind (Isa 6:9–10) to how big Yahweh really was—far bigger and more powerful than a tribal or national god could ever be.

His preaching the old Davidic covenant assurances in his early ministry he now saw was leading the people into the false confidence that God would take care of them no matter what. On the contrary, he had now to try to convince them that God was using Assyria to correct the king's and people's misunderstandings of God as a tribal deity: a result of the pervasive polytheistic thinking of the time. If Isaiah had preached that way earlier, God must have told him to do so. But in the light of the fall of Samaria, Isaiah was now certain that he had to unburden king and people of such false assurances and to instruct them in the fact that God was far more than a tribal or national deity obligated to protect them. One can appreciate how in exile a remnant recalled and reviewed Isaiah's and the other judgmental prophets' messages because, though they had been rejected back home, now in prison their messages made sense indeed. In polytheism Isaiah could have blamed the earlier deceptive message on a bad foreign god, a sort of Satan or devil. But if one believes truly in there being One God of All, then that is not a serious option.

It is not unlike the otherwise troublesome passages in Exod 7:3 and thirteen subsequent verses in which the text says that God hardened the heart of Pharaoh. These have long been troublesome to interpreters of the biblical text because they seem to contradict Moses's mission, but they are actually crucial for understanding the monotheizing process in the Bible, in which it is asserted that the good and the bad (from the viewpoint of the Israelites, of course) both stem from God. We moderns would, of course, have preferred that God soften the heart of Pharaoh and deliver an emancipation proclamation for the Hebrew slaves, and many have interpreted the verses to be grammatical problems because other verses use the reflexive form of the verb "harden" indicating that Pharaoh hardened his own heart. But in so wishing to absolve God of the tough stuff of life, we would have unknowingly made Pharaoh the hero of the exodus. Supposedly the slaves would have migrated out of Egypt peaceably and erected a stele of stones in honor of Pharaoh Ramses II, their liberator. But (and this is a big *but*) there would have been no Passover, no eating of the lamb in haste, no crossing the Reed Sea chased by Pharaoh's forces, and no story of salvation to tell the children for generations to come. No, God apparently understood Pharaoh's point of view. How was a responsible ruler of Egypt to let all that cheap labor just disappear in a cloud of good feeling for freeing the slaves? Cheap labor is what bolsters the rule of the privileged in any society.

Americans who supported the Confederacy and subsequently Jim Crow laws in the South would well have been able to appreciate Pharaoh's point of view, if they had been honest. It would be comparable to asking the Old South to liberate the African slaves and thus totally destroy its economy in a pen stroke, or asking segregationists in the South after the Civil War to abolish Jim Crow and integrate blacks and whites, and further wreck in their minds the economy of the recovering South that still depended on cheap black labor. Segregation and racism are still the pattern of much of the USA. The first took a brutal civil war and the second the determined efforts of far-sighted people a century later after the martyrdoms of Martin Luther King Jr. and of the Kennedy brothers. This is not to sympathize with slave owners or segregationists. Rather, it is to be realistic about humans, and how they have through history maltreated other humans in order to enrich themselves. No, the monotheizing process that the Bible describes in its history, from its origins to the stabilization of the biblical canon, is brutally realistic and faces the human condition as it truly is.

The theological point is that God was the God of the Egyptians and of the Confederacy, as well as of the slaves in both cases. President Lincoln pointedly said that North and South read the same Bible and prayed to the same God with opposing results. It is easy much later to condemn the slaveholders and the segregationists, but that is bad history as well as bad biblical interpretation. The Bible invites its readers to identify with the bad guys, those to whom the prophets and Jesus spoke, so that the readers' own sins, hubris, and arrogance can be exposed and hopefully avoided. For the Christian it means identifying with Judas Iscariot in reading the Passion Account so that our own current exceptionalist aspirations can be exposed—or, indeed, the sins of all the disciples according to Luke 22:21–52. It means understanding Judas's and the lethargic disciples' point of view: the disappointment that Jesus was not the kind of messiah they had expected. Judas apparently felt betrayed before he betrayed Jesus, who, in his young Zealot's nationalist mind, was but a messianic pretender. Christians ever since have vilified Judas and voided the Bible's message that the human condition is characterized by difference (including by the possibility that individuals may take different viewpoints on an issue). The truth, depicted in the Bible, that the human condition is marked by difference points to the Bible's mandate toward monotheism, toward one God for All.

In Isa 28:16 the prophet states that God was in his time about to resignify the purpose of a stone that, according to Sennacharib's plans taking shape beyond the city walls, was to be hurled against Jerusalem by the Assyrian siegework machines (2 Kings 18–20; Isaiah 36–38; 2 Chronicles 32; and esp. 2 Kgs 19:32). God would, Isaiah asserts, convert such an Assyrian siege stone into a precious cornerstone for a sure foundation of a Jerusalem later to be built on and around it. On the stone, Isaiah says, there would be an inscription that would read, "He who believes will not be in a frenzy." But the inscription can be read in two opposite ways. Either the inscription could mean that Yahweh would defend Jerusalem against Sennacherib despite the siege, and the one "who believes" would be confident that Yahweh could and would. Or the inscription could be read to mean that those who believe can be assured that God could turn even this pending disaster into a future blessing. The first meaning would support those who believed in their tribal Yahweh and the inviolability of Jerusalem; the second would support the monotheizing thrust of the prophetic message that God can turn disaster into a new beginning, a new building in place of the old—just as Joseph told his brothers that the evil they had done him God would convert into a blessing (Gen 50:20). Which meaning one assigned to the inscription depended on the hermeneutic (the top angle of the hermeneutic triangle) by which it was read.

If one still believed in Yahweh as a strong, powerful tribal or nationalist god, the inscription could be interpreted to mean that God would avert the Assyrian disaster. If one believed, with Isaiah, that nothing could escape God's judgments, not even exceptional Jerusalem, one even so also believed that God could transform the disaster the Assyrians were causing—and it indeed would be a disaster—into a new Jerusalem, a new Israel. That is what later happened with the Babylonian destruction of Jerusalem, hence the Isaianic version of the Deuteronomic history of the siege in Isaiah 39. If God is viewed as creator as well as redeemer, then God would be seen as able also to transform disaster into blessing. Out of it was born the new Israel, Judaism, from the ashes of the old.

The Monotheizing Process

The first hermeneutic stemmed from belief in God as a tribal redeemer god; the second stemmed from belief that God was both creator of all peoples and redeemer of all the world that God had created through the election of Israel—not for privilege but for service to the rest of creation (Gen 12:3). The second hermeneutic understood that God as both creator and redeemer, not just as redeemer, could wrest new life from death. If God could create in the first place, God could create again. The expansion of Israel's concept of deity before and during the exile from an intertribal or a national concept of God to the concept of a God of All—of both creator and redeemer—marked a transformative step in the monotheizing process.[7] It formed the base of Early Judaism out of which developed both Rabbinic Judaism and Christianity.

The other judgmental prophets all support this same understanding of the monotheizing process, especially Jeremiah in the decades before the Babylonian destruction of Jerusalem and the temple. Jeremiah in effect built on what the eighth-century prophets had proclaimed.[8] He undoubtedly had learned of the work of Amos and Hosea from refugees from the north, and in Jerusalem from Micah, and especially from the agonizing experience of Isaiah's learning on the job how powerful the monotheizing process was for his time. At Jeremiah's trial recorded in chapter 26, Mic 3:12 is quoted in Jeremiah's defense against those who indict him for blasphemy and sedition (Jer 26:18). Jeremiah goes so far as to claim that Nebuchadnezzar, the king of the enemy Babylon, is God's servant or ambassador, and that only by succumbing to him as God's agent would Judah be transformed (Jer 25:9; 27:6; 43:10). Jeremiah in his debate with Hananiah and in his comments about false prophecy, at least in the text as received (Jeremiah 23–29), makes it clear that the real distinction between true and false prophecy comes out in the monotheizing process because only through it could one understand that God would call

---

7. Sanders and Capetz, "*Credo in Unum Deum*." See Appendix.
8. Sanders, "The Book of Job."

Nebuchadnezzar his servant and use Nebuchadnezzar's imperial ambitions to crush and transform Judah.[9]

The Isaiah of the exile, then, nearly a century later in a prison camp in Babylon where he undoubtedly had learned of the process from disciples of the earlier prophets, called Cyrus, King of Persia, God's anointed messiah (Isa 45:1). Thus the monotheizing process was firmly launched. It was for the nascent Judaism that would be born out of the disaster to affirm belief in One God of All as the very basis of its truth—even though like Christianity, Islam and modern Judaism often act like ancient henotheistic cults but call themselves monotheistic.

It becomes clear after careful historical-critical reading of the Bible that the death-and-resurrection experience (which saw the complete dissolution of old Israel and Judah and yet out of it the birth of Early Judaism effected by the monotheizing process) is what instigated the idea of canon and induced the gradual acceptance in increasing, scattered Jewish communities of certain books and blocs of text as part of it.[10] The old Bronze- and Iron-Age traditions that survived the Late Iron Age holocaust of total destruction were those that could be adapted and edited so that (1) the disaster was sufficiently and effectively explained, and (2) an emerging priestly, temple-oriented new Israel after the exile was seen as a worthy heir, preserving those traditions in their new form. Nascent Early Judaism had also to explain how the greatly expanding ideas about Yahweh were rooted in those traditions that came to be seen as the launching pad for the monotheizing process.

But traditions were not the only survivors. A remnant of followers also survived and became the first adherents of Early Judaism. That the Prophetic Corpus comes in the Jewish canon, or Tanakh, immediately after the recital story from the Genesis promises through to the accounts of the destruction of ancient Israel and Judah in 2 Kings, was crucial to the argument of the remnant that survived the holocaust and became Early Judaism. Not

9. Sanders, "Hermeneutics of True and False Prophecy."

10. Sanders, *Torah and Canon* (2nd ed.), 95–103.

only had the prophets who became a part of the canon argued that the disaster entailed God's judgments on old Israel and Judah, but almost all these prophets also argued that God would wrest from the ashes of the old a new Israel. They used different metaphors to explain God's using the disaster to create a new people as heirs to the promises: divine discipline, purging (either by water or by fire—in biophysics fire as nature's sure agent for change and new life), refining, or surgery. Hosea, Jeremiah, and Ezekiel used the surgery metaphor in poignant ways.[11] Jeremiah and Ezekiel argued that God would suture his way of thinking (Torah) on the people's heart collectively (Jer 31:31–34), and Ezekiel that God would take out the old heart of stone and replace it with a new heart (Ezek 11:19; 36:26). Jeremiah used also the metaphor of a potter totally recasting the clay into a new form altogether (Jer 18:1–12). Only the One God of All could effect such transformation by Judah's enemy, Babylonia, God's agent or servant.

11. Sanders, "The Book of Job."

4

The Second Testament and the Monotheizing Process

Luke and Jubilee

Luke's gospel argues that Jesus was sent by God to fulfill the hope expressed in Isaiah 61 that God would send a herald to proclaim the year God had chosen to introduce the Jubilee (Luke 4:16–30). The concept of Jubilee has a long prehistory to the legislation found in Deuteronomy 15 and Leviticus 25. Those passages set aside a year for the forgiveness of all debts, for the release of slaves (indentured or jailed often to pay off debts) and for the repatriation of property (that had been sold to pay debts) to the original tribe to which God had assigned the given portion of the promised land as described in the Torah. In the Bible, a Jubilee year was set by royal proclamation, usually to raise an army (made difficult because of the power of an oligarchy to whom most people owed debts—see Jeremiah 34); but after the exile, the concept of Jubilee underwent transformation that resulted in different ways of observing Jubilee. It was taken out of the hands of both the king and the calendar (the province of the priests) and either was observed in the breach by the introduction of the *prosbul* (Mishnah *Shebi'ith* 10:3–7) or, pertinent to understanding Jesus's teachings and parables, was understood to occur whenever God would proclaim the year of *Shemitah* (Deuteronomy 15) or *Deror* (Leviticus 25): both words mean "release" or "forgiveness." It was the firm belief at Qumran that God would soon proclaim the Jubilee, not as a year of settling debts only, but as the future time when God would intervene in the miserable affairs of mankind and counter the evils of the world, especially the Roman occupation (11QMelchizedek).[1]

Luke's gospel may well be called "the Jubilee gospel" because throughout the gospel, and even in Acts, Jesus is understood to be the herald sent by God to proclaim God's Jubilee for the whole world. While Luke did not deny the messianic claims afoot about Jesus in his time, Luke was convinced that Jesus's ministry and message were best understood as heralding God's Jubilee for the world.

That indeed was the cause of the congregation's reaction at Nazareth already at the beginning of Jesus's ministry, according to Luke's gospel. In that sermon, God was proclaiming the ultimate Jubilee in Jesus's ministry. Jesus interpreted the all-important Jubilee passage in Isaiah 61 by reference to 1 Kings 17 and 2 Kings 5. In both these passages, God's messengers or prophets showed that God was the God of foreigners as well as of Israel. In 1 Kings 17 Elijah is saved by the sacrifice of a Sidonese widow, and in 2 Kings 5 Elisha heals an enemy army general. The poor Nazareth congregation needed relief from Roman taxation and release from Roman oppression generally. After Jesus had read the Haftarah (Prophets) portion for that Sabbath from Isaiah 61 (along with phrases from other Isaiah Jubilee passages), the Nazarenes fully expected that in his sermon Jesus would declare that God was coming to their aid and would release them from the Roman yoke (hence the favorable comments right after the reading). But after Jesus had preached on the Isaiah passages by reference to the missions of Elijah and Elisha to foreigners, the Nazareth congregation wanted to lynch him. They turned from doting neighbors into a hostile mob because of

---

1. Sanders, "From Isaiah 61 to Luke 4."

a sermon that said God cared for foreigners—even Romans—too. Luke was clearly a thoroughgoing monotheizer.

A number of the parables and sayings in Luke are based on the Jubilee concept of forgiveness of debts to God, which are human sins. When, for example in Luke 7, disciples of John the Baptist asked Jesus if he was the one who was to come, Jesus, with obvious patience, responded in the terms of Isa 61:1 and 58:6—the very passage he had read in the Nazareth synagogue—plus Isaiah 35: "Go tell John what you have seen and heard . . ." about the blind receiving their sight, the lame walking, and so forth. Then Luke closes the chapter with a parable about a woman who slipped into a banquet where Jesus was guest, bathed his feet with her tears, wiped them with her hair, kissed them, and anointed them with expensive ointment. Since she was known to the host and others as a woman of the street, they said to themselves, *If he were really a prophet, he'd know what kind of woman she was.* Jesus, apparently knowing their inner thoughts, told a Jubilee story of a creditor who forgave two debtors, and then Jesus forgave the woman her sins. It was clearly a Jubilee story underlining the theme set in the Nazareth sermon; but since the religious folk around the table were not convinced or did not know that Jesus was introducing God's Jubilee, they missed the point of Jesus's forgiving the woman's sins, which were many. Forgiveness of human sin is forgiveness of debts to God, the theological message of Jubilee.[2] Jesus did not condemn the woman because of her profession. He instead showed deep understanding of her plight as a human being.

Even the Great Banquet parable in Luke 14:15–24 echoes the Jubilee theme. While it resignifies the acceptable excuses for avoiding fighting in a holy war, as listed in Deuteronomy 20 (reasons with which those who considered themselves *keklemenoi* or "invited" opted out of the banquet), the parable is a dynamic sequel to the Jubilee theme. They knew they could not participate in the victory banquet reserved for those who had fought in the holy war and rightly refrained from accepting the invitation to the feast. Those who were urged to come in and enjoy the banquet

2. Sanders, "Sins, Debts, and Jubilee Release."

would have been those who (whether or not they knew their sins were forgiven because they believed that the Jubilee had by Jesus's ministry been introduced for all) were not required to know about the holy war and the victory. The *keklemenoi*, or those who felt confident they were the elect, simply opted out of the Jubilee celebrations; they after all felt they had no debts to God![3] The dispossessed apparently had no such self-deception and were ushered in to enjoy the victory banquet.

The central theme of Jubilee was that the land—indeed all creation—belongs to God, the Giver of all and anything that humans have. Jubilee puts in perspective the patent absurdity of humans' thinking they own anything of God's creation—land or otherwise (Matt 19:21–26). They might hold things in trust for a lifetime, but they belong to God. Jesus then concludes his teachings in Luke 14 with the statement that one must renounce all that one has in order to be his disciple. To understand renunciation of all one has is to recognize that it was all God's gift in the first place. The difficulty humans have in following Jesus's views about wealth is recognized in his teachings. The concepts of ownership and property are illusions humans embrace that shield us from the truth of human beingness. The truth of the expression that the love of money is the root of all evil eludes the successful and the honored in normal society; their wealth and the honor in which society holds them blind them to God's truth. It is difficult for society's honored to understand Jesus's saying that it is as difficult for a rich person to enter the kingdom of God's truth as it is for a camel to go through a needle's eye. Luke follows up (in chapter 15) with three parables about what humans hold dear: the lost sheep, the lost coin, and the lost son. Each is recovered, causing great joy, and not a little consternation on the part of those who think they own and deserve what they have. Luke caps this with a story about a steward who knows he only manages the owner's possessions (Luke 16:1–9) and with another about the rich who fool themselves into thinking they are honorable (Luke 16:19–31). When they want to know how to inherit eternal life, Jesus again stresses

3. Sanders, "The Ethic of Election in Luke's Great Banquet Parable."

that one must renounce what one thinks one owns and give it all to the poor (Luke 18:18–25).

One might well ask why the Bible so often insists that God is partial to the poor. And the reason is never too hard to find: the rich and those who pride themselves that they are honored (footing the bills for beautiful edifices of worship) are in constant danger of loving not God, the Giver of all gifts, but what God has given them: this is the basic meaning of idolatry. North American and European societies, which became wealthy on the backs of Africans, Asians, and First Americans, shielded by their wealth, find it difficult to understand the revolt of the rest of the world against Western dominance. To avert the discomfort of Jesus's teachings, we Western Christians imagine idolatry as something ancient Canaanites did in worshiping Baal, not what we do daily. Or we engage in blatant idolatry of Jesus as *our* Christ instead of worshiping God, who creates and blesses with gifts untold, including God's Christ, God's most precious gift.

When Jesus and the disciples in Luke approach the city and the temple, Luke dramatically shows Jesus and his disciples reenacting a psalm it was forbidden to reenact, as it had been back when Israel had kings: Psalm 118.[4] Because the religious authorities do not agree that the Jubilee had been introduced or that Jesus was the anointed herald/messiah come to proclaim it, they begin to denounce Jesus. Jesus then debates a number of points of Scripture with the authorities, who become more and more concerned that he is going to provoke the ire of the Roman occupation, and seek to silence him. The Passion account moves along then, with Luke demonstrating Jesus's knowledge of Scripture, interpreting it in ways the religious authorities renounce, again out of fear of the Romans.

Luke then closes his gospel, after the resurrection-story account, with a story unique to Luke—about two followers of Jesus in despair making their way home to Emmaus. Luke provides a kind of climax to his gospel-length interpretation of all the Jesus events as the introduction of God's Jubilee for all people by

4. Sanders, "A Hermeneutic Fabric."

depicting a scene of table fellowship in Cleopas's Emmaus home, in which Jesus "opened" eyes by "opening" the Scriptures (Luke 24:13–33). Luke indulges a solecism in recounting the scene by using the same word for opening the eyes as for opening Scripture. The message Luke undoubtedly wanted to convey was that it was by opening Scripture (echoing the account of the sermon at Nazareth in Luke 4:17 where the proper word for opening a scroll was used) that one's eyes are opened to see what God is doing in and through Jesus's ministry. How else is one to know about the Jubilee and all it implied for what God was doing in and through Jesus? Jubilee was observed at the time only by default, in the practice of *prosbul,* a waiver that exempted any and all from actually obeying Jubilee. One needed to know the importance of God's proclamation of the Jubilee in Isaiah 61 truly to understand all that Jesus had done. In the Jubilee, God is truly acknowledged to be the One God of All. The Christian doctrine of redemption would have had its origins in the concept of Jubilee.

Matthew and the One God

Matthew's gospel, while it does not so obviously base Jesus's message on the Jubilee theme, comes to full fruition if a monotheizing hermeneutic is used in reading it. If one reads the Sermon on the Mount (Matthew 5–7) understanding *markarios,* often translated "blessed" or "happy" rather as "honored" and its opposite as "shamed," then one perceives the Sermon as a direct challenge to the honor/shame syndrome that has been a social contract, as it were, for centuries in most human societies, even and especially today in capitalist societies.[5] The syndrome clearly implies that those who are wealthy or famous in popular terms have been and are usually highly honored in most societies from antiquity to today. The concept of meritocracy, after the Enlightenment, was supposed to challenge the older social classes, each ordained by God to fulfill their respective roles to make society work. But meri-

5. Hanson, "'How Honorable!' 'How Shameful!': A Cultural Analysis of Matthew's Makarisms and Reproaches."

tocracy has since been co-opted by the syndrome, which continues unabated.

Jesus challenges the syndrome radically and declares in no uncertain terms that in God's economy or realm the opposite will be true: for in God those who use up their lives making the rich richer will be honored whereas those who are now lauded by society will be shamed. Luke makes this point as clearly as any in Matthew with his story about the rich man and Lazarus, the poor man who dedicated his life to doing menial jobs for the rich man, making him richer while Lazarus remained destitute (Luke 16). Jesus makes it shockingly clear that in God's economy, when both the rich man and Lazarus have died, it will be Lazarus who will receive the honor God (not human society) bestows, but not the rich man, who will be shocked by the God's truth about economic justice.

Matthew and Luke make essentially the same points about economic justice but often with different Jesus traditions to express them. If one reads the Sermon on the Mount using a monotheizing hermeneutic, then the admonition to love one's enemies comes as a rousing climax and no surprise: one comes close to being god-like, indeed *telos* (that is to say, perfect) like God, when one loves one's enemies, that is, understands their point of view instead of denigrating it in order to argue one's own. Why? Because God, who created and creates all beings, understands both sides of our pitiful human conflicts. Does this mean that one never struggles— as in true *jihad* that the Qur'an mandates—for what one believes is right? No, but the struggles of one side take on far greater meaning if the members on that side are fully aware of and even respect perspectives of their opponents and still engage in the struggle. When humans refuse to demonize opponents in these struggles, then progress is made in the struggle itself before any outcome might settle it.

Matthew's form of the dominical prayer in Matt 6:9–13 is even more of a Jubilee prayer than the parallel in Luke 11:2–4, for in Matthew the word that Luke has for "sins" is rendered "debts":

that which is to be forgiven or released in the Jubilee.[6] Luke makes clear that debts to God are sins, and it is appropriate that at that point in the Lukan gospel (at the beginning of the trek to Jerusalem in Luke's central section) one should ask God to forgive one's debts to God. One should ask God to forgive debts because in the Jubilee, creditors commit to forgive all those indebted to them. However, even more than the Lukan version, the Matthean version of the Lord's Prayer—particularly with its use of the word "debts" for "sins"—underscores beyond a reasonable doubt that the Jubilee theme undergirds Matthew's gospel. Matthew's form of the prayer asks of God to forgive the solicitor's sins or debts to God, because in Jubilee the petitioner commits to release all debts incurred. This connection between the Jubilee and the Lord's Prayer in both Luke and Matthew assumes that the one praying to God for forgiveness is a human being who understands what it is like to be a debtor to other human beings. Finally, as the gospels of Matthew and Luke came to be written, read, and heard, in a manifestation of Jubilee forgiveness, God was using Rome to transform Early Judaism into Christianity and rabbinic Judaism. In the same way, God had employed Assyrian and Babylonian imperialism six centuries earlier to transform old Israel and Judah into Early Judaism.

Jesus goes on to say that we should be as perfect as God in heaven is perfect (Matt 5:48). How so? How could we possibly become as perfect as God is? The point of the passage is that we can be and will become "perfect" (*telos*) if we strive to understand the humanity, fears, and hopes of others, even our enemies. The Matthean passage may have been derived from the early so-called Q source (cf. Luke 6:27–31). With the Lukan passage, it is the most monotheizing in the whole Bible. It got Jesus into deep trouble in his time, just as monotheizing in their time had gotten the prophets in trouble—and usually gets monotheizers into trouble today, especially with church doctrine. What does *telos*, the Greek word behind the translation "perfect," mean in the Matthean passage? *Telos* can mean "goal," "purpose," "end," and finally "perfect," or "complete"—the basic meaning of the English word *perfect*, and

6. Oakman, *Jesus, Debt, and the Lord's Prayer.*

therefore a good translation in the context. What would complete like God be or mean? I submit that it meant and means what the fuller passage itself says about God: understanding both sides of all human conflicts, precisely loving the enemy (even hardening the heart of Pharaoh?), as Jesus commands at the beginning of the pericope, but with a bias for the powerless. In other words, to love God with all the heart, self, and means (the *Shema'*) is to strive to understand those who hold positions other than our own, to understand them as being as human, limited, and frail as we ourselves. This is the hermeneutic the Bible requires for understanding it thoroughly, a monotheizing hermeneutic in a historical-critical mode. God is bigger than we think—indeed, than anybody can think.

5

What Monotheizing Would Mean Today

The Bible offers from the earliest traditions to the latest a launching pad from which the three so-called Abrahamic religions should, if faithful to their origins, continue the monotheizing process.

For Judaism, belief in and practice of monotheizing would mean recasting its ancient liturgies to eliminate those recitals and prayers that continue to praise God as "our God" and "the God of our ancestors" in order rather to express (as some of the prayers already do) the belief that God is the One God of All. In this recasting, the liturgy would further acknowledge that despite all the suffering that the West and Christianity have caused Jews since Constantine, it insists on believing that God is the One God of All, and it extends that belief to its treatment of Palestinians, whose ancestral and personal homes are now theirs. This would mean modifying the ideals of Jewish nationalism to reflect that firm belief and to restrain it from overwhelming Judaism, as it did ancient Israel and Judah. Finally, Israel would be the Palestinians' best friend since the Palestinians have no other in the world of Realpolitik, and Israel would show the world out of its true Judaism the real meaning of belief that God is One and the God of All. It has been two thousand years since Jews had to deal with their own nationalism, and almost three thousand since the prophets denounced its excesses. Indeed, one wonders if modern Jewish nationalism developed out of an understandable impatience with waiting for the messiah.

For Islam, openly based in large part on Judaism and Christianity, it would mean truly believing that God has spoken and speaks through many modes and cultures in divine attempts to reach all peoples—whether through Muslim doctrines and traditions or through others—and to cease and desist from condemning others often called infidels. It would mean attempting to understand how and why Judaism to a limited degree and Christianity pervasively became infused with Hellenism and seem so foreign to many present-day Muslims.

For Christianity, belief and practice in the monotheizing process would mean recasting its ancient liturgies to eliminate those recitals and prayers that continue to exalt Christianity as the only way to approach God or believe in God, to eliminate all vestiges of (Barthian) christocentric theism, and to engage in efforts to understand what a theocentric Christology would truly mean for church and world. Some Western Christians, including the Roman Church, have begun to confess that God has never abrogated the covenant with Judaism; that is a beginning step. Monotheizing would require restudying what the Gospels say about Christ in terms of belief that God is the One God of all humankind. When I tried this starting with the Gospel of Luke and then Matthew, meanings emerged that fairly made the Gospels glisten and shine as I had never before experienced. Monotheizing would mean ceasing and desisting from attempts to exalt Western cultural understandings of Christianity that do not exalt God at all but exalt limited cultural understandings of who *our* Christ was and is. It would mean serious requestioning of anything in Christian theology that is self-serving in any way. And it would surely mean returning to what the Gospels say Jesus, the ultimate monotheizing Jew, taught, and attempting seriously to teach and preach his good news, and not the gospel we have professed in order to support our biases and prejudices. The emerging theocentric gospel would shame the Christian from using the Bible and the gospel to support racism, bigotry, homophobia, or misogyny. Shielding modern prejudice behind a few select biblical verses while ignoring the many verses inconvenient to obey would cease completely. For all three monotheistic faiths, true montheizing would mean learning not only from each other but from others, faith-based or not.

Revelation is central to all three religions, but it has tragically allowed many theologians of each to claim exclusivity for their understandings of faith. It has been changed among many Christians from understanding what God has done in and through Christ for the whole world to claims of exclusivity and privilege for members. The Apostle Paul's writings focus in his Gentile mission on faith as the sole condition to being in Christ and not adherence to the law. Paul took this focus in order to minimize obstacles to those in the Greco-Roman world convinced of the message of the new Jewish gospel so that they not have to be circumcised or give up favorite foods. His reducing the importance of cultural traits in the Greco-Roman world in order for non-Jews to express their faith in what God had done and was doing in Christ brought inordinate emphasis on the rightness of faith and how it was expressed. Then when Constantine became Christian (nominally or otherwise), that emphasis in Christian orthodoxy became a vicious tool to persecute those who failed to say the right words in order to escape martyrdom at the hands of Christians. In other words, after Constantine, the newly powerful Christians turned around and did to Jews and others precisely what they had suffered under earlier Roman rule. They also denounced most forms of dissent as heresy in order to eradicate dialogue and so deny that the Holy Spirit was challenging their distortions of the gospel.[1]

The Christianization of the Roman world was undoubtedly the worst thing that had happened to Jews to that point (so some Jewish thinkers say)—worse than the later Holocaust under Hitler, which was its ultimate, most vicious outcome, and it boded ill for anybody who refused to become Christian, because of the claims of exclusivity on the part of Christian leaders in their

---

1. Sanders, "Canon as Dialogue."

continuing tribal cast of the Christian movement. Some of the New Testament appears to make claims of exclusivity, and those passages, which need to be understood in their original contexts, have been self-servingly used to bolster claims for contemporary forms of Christianity at any given period of Christian history. But if the Holy Spirit has been understood to lead the church out of ancient cultural traps and trappings of the First Testament into the world of enlightenment, science, and technology, can it not also be understood to lead the church away from the deep-seated sin of self-serving claims based on a few New Testament passages? Can Christians not instead understand God's work in Christ to be precisely that, namely, God's work in *God's* Christ and not the work of a *Christian* Christ—particularly when the doctrine of the incarnation has been used by Christians to make claims for humans who profess it rather than as occasion for praising God? Christians must always remind themselves that Jesus was not a Christian and that God is not a Christian.

The churches must move from their present focus on (Barthian) christocentric theology to a theocentric Christology in which the focus would be on the One God of All that we all profess we believe in, and not on our understandings of what God has done in *our* Christ. And once we have done that, we must remember that God is incomprehensible and inscrutable, beyond all human claims to know God. Hosea's and other prophets' urging "to know the LORD" did not and cannot mean having exhaustive knowledge of all that God is. The inherent wisdom of the words Moses heard from the burning bush is central to biblical thought—"I am that I am" (Exod 3:14)—and admits of no attempt to shackle concepts of God with any predicate to the verb *I am*. No religion can exhaustively know God, none. Religions of the world get glimpses of what God is like and should share them with each other rather than make self-serving and privileged claims about God. The greater that human focus is on the otherness and ineffableness of God, the greater is human humility.

The Enlightenment was a gift of God in due season and brought humans to the astounding insights of science about God's amazing creation.[2] We now know that the small rock we inhabit spinning around the sun is but a tiny part of a vast, ever expanding multiverse. We now know that there are at least ten dimensions to God's vast creation over against which to measure the pitiful three-dimensional world common sense says we grasp as truth. Nearly every advance in implementing the insights of the Enlightenment has been fought by most churches, and God has had to work through secular institutions to effect his will.[3] Christianity has come dangerously close to idolatry in adoring Christ instead of God in Christ. Instead of worshiping our Christ, we Christians should worship and adore God and not any of God's gifts, not even God's greatest gift in Jesus Christ. Christians need to stop and ask why Jews and Muslims and others resist conversion. Just as the prophets reread the national epic story of the Exodus–Wanderings–Entrance through the prism of international wisdom, so Jesus reread Scripture through the Hellenized wisdom of the first century CE. In this perspective the Bible is a paradigm that provides the means whereby adherents today can learn to conjugate the verbs of God's activity in the world and decline the nouns of the majesty and grace of the One God of All.

The more we humans learn of God's incomprehensible nature and of the fact that God cannot be contained in any theological box that humans want to put God in, the greater must be human humility in discourse about God. None of us gets it right, not because God has not tried in grace and in varied ways to reach out to us humans, but because we humans have been wont to try to trap God in human, pitiful understandings of that grace. The Bible and the Qur'an seem to delight in challenging humans with principles hard for us to follow, whether it be the concept that God (not the wealthy among us) owns all God created, the concept of Jubilee that we have never seemed to fathom, or the command to monotheize our lives. Maybe we just aren't equipped to handle the God's truth. Einstein and even Hawking use the word *God* to express their broader visions. Most use the word *nature*, uncomfortable

2. Weis and Carr, eds., *A Gift of God.*
3. Sanders, "God's Work in the Secular World."

with using a theological term—as though Nature were a force, like a god comfortable to appeal to.

To resume the monotheizing process and attempt to be obedient to its mandate may seem more than mere humans can manage. Indeed Jesus went on to say that we should strive to be perfect as God is perfect, but the passage in Matthew 5 says clearly that this means like God, appreciating both sides of all our conflicts on this small planet, as God did already in the exodus events. To monotheize is no more utopian than (for Jews) expecting the messiah or indeed (for Christians) the second coming of Christ. Jesus's bidding to love the enemy has been dismissed as utopian and unrealistic. But seen as the culmination of the monotheizing process, it means that all humans must at least learn to appreciate the enemy's situation, position, and point of view, lest we all become our own worst enemies on this pitifully shrinking planet.

The Bible—both testaments—and indeed Islam claim that the One God who casts up the valadium vaults and puts the planets into their orbits stoops in love and grace to human levels of existence in incomprehensible and inscrutable love. To believe in such a message induces incomparable measures of humility and gratitude and the necessity to reach out to each other on this ever-shrinking speck of cosmic dust we inhabit. Such a message prompts us to cease and desist from any human claim that would belittle the incomparable majesty and the incomprehensible grace of the One God of us all. The monotheizing process that the Bible and the Qur'an launched is the first and basic commandment on which all else depends, as the rabbis and the imams have poignantly taught: to love God with all we have and are, and to love our earthly neighbors—even our enemies—as we do ourselves is the monotheizing process.

Appendix

Credo in Unum Deum

A Challenge

with Paul E. Capetz

BELIEF IN ONE GOD is as intrinsic and integral to the Christian faith as it is to Judaism and Islam. But none of the three has yet arrived at accountable belief in the One God of All. Each is to some extent still caught in the ephemeral cultural traps and trappings in which the Scriptures and traditions of each were written. And each has remained in its comfort zone of henotheism (belief in its particular view of God), falling well short of true monotheism, which recognizes that God is incomprehensible.[1]

Some adherents of Christianity falsely think that some of those cultural trappings are traits of monotheism—such as patriarchalism and the honor/shame syndrome on which nearly all societies are and have been structured. Some have worked to eliminate the trappings but have kept henotheism intact—or worse, have foolishly toyed with the chaos of polytheism. Belief in the One God of All has at best been held out, like the coming of Messiah

1. See Capetz, *God: A Brief History.*

62

or the second coming of Christ, as a goal worth aspiring to. But at the same time the goal of common belief in the One God of All is called unrealistic and unattainable. It is our contention, on the contrary, that the time has come for all three religions (Judaism, Christianity, and Islam) to work out what belief in the integrity of reality and of all humanity really means in contemporary terms, and to strive to make that belief a reality if humanity is to survive the twenty-first century.

When in the late second century the emerging orthodox or catholic churches rejected Marcion's call to jettison the Scriptures of Judaism and to replace them with a canon of distinctively Christian writings (*New Testament* or *Second Testament*), this was no mere editorial decision about which books deserve to be included in the Bible. Rather, this decision to retain the Scriptures of Early Judaism as integral to the church's Bible was perhaps the most momentous decision up to that time regarding the religious and theological identity of the new religion to be called Christianity. Had the decision gone in Marcion's favor, the church not only would have lost its claim to stand in faithful continuity with the religious tradition of ancient Israel, but also would have forfeited its fundamental presupposition of monotheism that has since exercised a measure of constraint on how all the other doctrines of Christian faith—such as Christology and soteriology—have been interpreted.

Marcion and his followers were not monotheists. Like the gnostics to whom they have often been compared, they were dualists. But unlike the metaphysical dualism of gnosticism, which pits the creator deity of this evil material world against the good redeemer deity who redeems our good spirits from their imprisonment in physical bodies, the Marcionite dualism was of a soteriological sort and based on a radicalizing distortion of the distinction between faith and works wielded by the Apostle Paul. For Marcion, therefore, the deity revealed by Jesus is a God of grace, whereas the deity attested by the Jewish Bible is a God of righteousness. By its categorical rejection of all forms of dualism and its concomitant embrace of the Scriptures of Judaism in a double-testament Bible, the church affirmed the same basic tenet that Jews have proclaimed throughout the centuries: "Hear, O Israel, the LORD our God is one." In theological terms, this affirmation means that the one God is creator, judge, and redeemer. Since God is the ultimate source of both matter and spirit, material reality cannot be pitted against spiritual reality as though the former were evil and the latter good: "God saw all that he had made and, behold, it was very good" (Gen 1:31). Because God is good, everything God has made is good.

The source of evil in the world is human sin, which has its root in a misuse of freedom by creatures made in the image of God. We are not compelled to sin because we live in an evil material world, as dualists imagine. Putting the point of the verse from Genesis in a more philosophical vein, Augustine affirmed the maxim: *esse qua esse bonum est* (whatever exists is good simply by virtue of its existence). To the extent that something can also be described as evil, it must be understood that evil can be nothing other than a corruption of a finite good, since a completely evil entity is a contradiction in terms, given the monotheistic premise. H. Richard Niebuhr later reformulated the same insight when he said that "the principle of being is the principle of value." Whatever has been created by God has value simply because God values it.[2]

The decision to retain Israel's Scriptures in the church placed Christianity squarely on the side of Judaism in its polemics against polytheistic religions. From the perspective of Jewish and Christian monotheists, worship of anything other than the one creator-redeemer God is idolatry since it reveres some aspect of God's world as though it were divine. This is why the early Christians were persecuted. Called atheists by the Romans because of their refusal to venerate the Roman pantheon, Christians, like Jews, certainly could not worship the emperor—a mere human being!—as a god. But there were other respects in which Christianity was different from Judaism. The first Jewish followers of Jesus believed that he was the promised messiah (Christ) of Israel. Other Jews could not

2. Niebuhr, *Radical Monotheism*; see also Gustafson, *Ethics from a Theocentric Perspective*.

accept this affirmation on account of the apparently nonmessianic fate of Jesus's crucifixion by the Romans. What was originally an intra-Jewish debate eventuated in a division between two religions represented by the synagogue and the church. Christians and Jews were as heated in their polemics against one another as both were toward the pagans. It is here that the central ambiguity emerged regarding the Christian appropriation of the Jewish Scriptures. The Christians claimed that the Jews did not understand their own Scriptures to the extent that they failed to recognize Jesus as the fulfillment of Israel's messianic hope. For their part, the Jews accused Christians of falsifying the plain meaning of texts in their shared scriptural canon so that those texts could be interpreted as pointing to Jesus.

Here we witness contrasting hermeneutical principles at work in the exegesis of texts that mirror the contrast between the hermeneutics of Marcion and that of the anti-Marcionite church. Marcion had insisted upon a literal reading of the texts in the light of the relevant historical and philological criteria for interpreting the meaning of a passage. The orthodox churches, however, rejected Marcion's demand for a literal or historical exegesis in favor of a spiritual or allegorical exegesis. Marcion agreed with the Jews that the Scriptures of the synagogue do not prophesy the coming of Jesus. For that reason it cannot be said that in its decision to include the Jewish Scriptures in the Christian Bible, the orthodox church adequately responded to Marcion's challenge. It did so only in part. It was not until the advent of historical-critical scholarship in the late eighteenth century and its general acceptance in the nineteenth century that the christological veneer was stripped away, and Israel's Scriptures began to be understood historically and developmentally in their ancient contexts. The new scholarly conclusions that resulted were, however, no less of a challenge to some traditional Jewish ways of interpreting the Bible than they were to inherited Christian modes of interpretation. That has reopened the question as to the religious and theological significance of this shared scriptural canon today, and the resurgence of Islam on the world stage has in effect forced a new look at the meaning of monotheism today.

The Canonical Process

We believe that the challenge perennially posed by the First Testament in its witness to developing monotheism is in danger of being lost in those very religious communities that claim this scriptural canon as sole base of authority. We are convinced that neither Judaism nor Christianity in its present forms can be described as consistently monotheistic in outlook and practice. But since we are Christians and not Jews, we shall focus our critical and constructive efforts in this essay on the churches. What follows, then, is a consideration of this challenge viewed from the perspective of current biblical scholarship with an eye toward its implications for Christian theology and ethics.

A cursory reading indicates that many in ancient Israel were polytheists, building altars to local gods, appealing to many gods, worshiping Baal or El or other regional deities. The many names used for the One God indicate that early on there were many gods in ancient Israel's life. Recent archaeological studies indicate indeed that Yahweh (the most common name for Israel's God) had a consort, or wife.[3] This is so much the case that we cannot call the First Testament monotheistic, as though it contained a philosophical affirmation to that effect. What we should say, rather, is that the Bible—both Testaments—is a monotheizing literature. Late in the exilic period, Yahweh was viewed as both male and female (e.g., Isa 49:15). Hence the one God was viewed as both male and female, and neither. All metaphors used for God are inept and misleading and must not be absolutized. The process whereby Israel's ancient beliefs in numerous gods transformed into belief in the One God of All is what the First Testament provides, and it does so in amazing and stunning ways.

3. See Dever, *Did God Have a Wife?*

By the time Judaism arose late in the Iron Age out of the ashes and defeat of the old kingdoms of Israel and Judah, it affirmed belief in One Yahweh. The book of Deuteronomy is clear about this in the *Shema'* (Deut 6:4–5): "Hear, O Israel, Yahweh our God is one Yahweh . . ." The meaning would have been clear by the time some arrived back in Palestine from the Babylonian exile. By that time all Jews claimed they believed in Yahweh, but the Deuteronomists (of the immediately preceding preexilic period) and those who followed their way of thinking in exile wanted to make clear that there was only one concept of Yahweh; Jews couldn't claim different concepts of Yahweh. If they were to survive, the one thing they all had to affirm was that there was only one Yahweh. Prior to that, different factions could claim that their concept of the national deity was the right one (e.g., in Joshua 24). Now that they were decimated and threatened with extinction, the priests, sages, and scribes of Early Judaism knew that their very survival depended on their commonly shared concept of One Yahweh.

While that may not yet have been what we now understand monotheism to mean, it was the foundation upon which it evolved; it provided the process by which it would develop. What happened to the remnant in the prisoner-of-war camps in ancient Babylonia provided the next step in the process. What is meant by *remnant* is precisely those Jews in exile who still recited some of the old preexilic stories about what Yahweh had done to and for Israel (e.g., Deut 26:5–9; 1 Sam 12:6–8), and who recalled with both pain and awe what the preexilic prophets had said about Yahweh being the God of their enemies as well. Many in exile, according to the biblical record (Isa 46:5–13 and so forth), did not care to remember the old stories. They assimilated to Babylonian culture and lost their identity. But enough of a remnant did remember so that they experienced a transformed continuity with the past. In rehearing the various preexilic prophets' words recited by their disciples in those camps over the seventy years of exile, the exiles realized that the prophets whom they had spurned in the old, prewar days had actually provided the path for them out of disaster into a new life. That new life, the old Israel transformed in the crucible of the exile, we call Judaism. Judaism would not be a nationalist cult like the old Yahwism in preexilic days but would be an international religion embracing the remnant wherever they were scattered throughout the new Persian Empire that defeated the Babylonian just after the middle of the sixth century BCE.

What had the prophets said that provided the destitute in exile with the power to survive, albeit in a new and more viable form? Herein lies the principal key to the monotheizing process.

The Prophets

Egypt had held hegemony over the Iron-Age kingdoms of Israel and Judah after Solomon's reign over the united kingdom in Jerusalem until the rise of the neo-Assyrian Empire in the middle of the eighth century BCE. Assyria was the first real threat to Egyptian dominance in the area, and it boded ill for Israel. So much so that a prophet, Amos, who lived in Tekoa down in Judah felt compelled to journey to Bethel up in Israel where there was a royal sanctuary. He was actually a shepherd and a dresser of sycamore trees, and had no ostensible authority to do what he was about to do. But his conviction was so strong that alone he took the situation in hand and appeared one morning in about 750 BCE at the sanctuary there. A large crowd had gathered to celebrate a sacred day on which they were convinced Yahweh would make an appearance to bless all they had done in his name under the reign of King Jeroboam II and to keep them safe from the Assyrians. The prophet Amos had no credentials and certainly was not expected to be a part of the proceedings that day.

But at just the right moment he spoke out in a loud voice exclaiming how God was going to judge their neighbor Syria for numerous transgressions. He thundered forth, "For the three transgressions and the four of Damascus . . ." He was specific then about their sins and the punishment Yahweh would mete out to the Syrians, Israel's old and hated enemy. While he had no authority, and though he certainly had a funny southern accent, what he was saying so far was just what the people had come to hear. Yahweh was against their neighbors, their enemies. They heard him out as he went on in the name of their God, Yahweh, to indict the Philistine cities, then Tyre and Sidon, followed by the Edomites, the Ammonites, the Moabites, and even their erstwhile cousins in Judah, whom they hated almost as much as the Syrians because of the corvée labor to which Jerusalem had subjected them under Solomon. In fact, Amos specified that the sin of Judah was in failing to adhere to the Torah of Yahweh. He surely got that right, they would have thought!

So far so good. We can be sure he had their rapt attention! But Amos then went on in the same rhetorical rhythm and cadences to indict the northern kingdom itself! But whereas the indictments against the peoples round about Israel had been for acts of inhumanity against neighboring peoples, Amos proceeded to say that Yahweh was indicting Israel for its inhumanity to its own people, its maltreatment of the poor in their own land. Good preaching had obviously turned into meddling!

The truly interesting thing about Amos's sermon (Amos 1:3—3:2), however, was the base of authority he offered for what he was saying (Amos 2:9-12). He recited the precious national story that Israel loved to recite in its claim to be God's special people, but he did so to contrast what Israel was doing to the poor at home with what Yahweh had done for them when they were slaves in Egypt. Yahweh, he affirmed, was their liberator from Egyptian bondage, their guide for forty years in the wilderness, and giver of the land they called home.

But when they had a chance on their own turf to do as Yahweh had done for their ancestors, they imitated Pharaoh instead of acting the way Yahweh had shown them: they oppressed the weak in their own land. The rich were getting richer, and the poor poorer. For this, Amos made clear that they would experience destitution and destruction beyond belief. He concluded his sermon by affirming Israelite belief that they were indeed the only family on earth God knew. But, Amos said, therefore Yahweh would punish them for all their sins (3:1-2). No one apparently had ever pointed out this formidable truth, and the Israelites at Bethel were not ready for it. Whether Amos's hearers were ready depended on their view of God, who was thought by most to be *their* god and would, of course, take care of them. But Amos, probably influenced by the wisdom movement in Tekoa (cf. 2 Samuel 14), proclaimed a view of Yahweh that was international, as the creator of all. For his trouble Amos was deported and ordered to go back home where he belonged. He was persona non grata for telling the truth about God. This was the fate of nearly all the preexilic prophets. He was the first of several prophets to appear over the next century and a half to insist that Israel's chosenness for a mission brought heavy responsibilities, and that *their* God was the God also of their neighbors and enemies all around them. Amos made it quite clear that while God had indeed brought them out of Egypt, God had also brought the Philistines from Caphtor and the Syrians from Kir (Amos 9:7). The other prophets' messages would be no more to the people's liking than Amos's had been. It was hard to hear that the true God was not theirs, not like a precious possession who knew the job description.

Israel had no idea at the time of the truth Amos was telling. He was deported back to Judah, but he was followed in the north by Hosea, who uttered in other words very much the same message. In the south, in Judah, after northern Israel fell to Assyria, Isaiah and Micah followed in the south (with messages similar to those of Amos and Hosea) during the eighth-century turmoil that accompanied the rise of Assyria. The same kind of truth was declaimed in the south in the seventh century by Zephaniah, Jeremiah, Habakkuk, and others during the rise and threat of the neo-Babylonian Empire.

If people at the time did not like what these prophets said, then why are the messages of these prophets the ones preserved in the Bible? Why don't we have the words of the popular prophets at the time, such as Hananiah (Jeremiah 28), who preached the good-old polytheism or henotheism that Judah warmly believed to be true? Yahweh was *their* God, and any other message was blasphemy according to the popular preachers.[4] Jeremiah was tried

4. Sanders, "The Challenge of Fundamentalism."

twice for preaching such "blasphemy" (Jeremiah 26 and 38), and Jesus was in his time as well.

What this "goodly fellowship of the prophets" said came true in historical fact—not necessarily the details, but the overall message. This was the main reason these particular prophetic works were later remembered and became a part of the enduring canon or Bible of Judaism. More than that, what above all came true was their insistence that Yahweh was not just Israel and Judah's national god. He was God of all peoples and not just theirs to petition and placate. In 722 BCE northern Israel was conquered by Assyria, and by 586 BCE southern Judah and Jerusalem were conquered and destroyed by Babylonia. In 722 many refugees from the north fled to Judah, which barely survived the Assyrian assault, but by the beginning of the sixth century the whole experiment of the Israel called and shaped in the books of Genesis and Exodus was nearly obliterated. The only hope for any kind of survival lay then with the prisoners of war in the camps in Babylonia, those we mentioned earlier, who began in those camps to recite the old stories and to recall what those awful prophets had said, whom they had rejected back in the prewar days.

It was through those recollections and memories that Judaism emerged in the exile to start anew with a transformed appreciation of who Yahweh was. The messages of the prophets they had hated now were the only ones that had meaning and provided hope. It began to become starkly clear that polytheism worked for the comfortable but had no validity and no truth during life's real crises. Polytheism, even henotheism, provides gods to love and gods to hate (including foreign gods and devils), but in a real crisis you did not want to hear that the bad gods had beaten your good god(s).

Most of the preexilic prophets also had said that the judgment or punishment with which God was afflicting them had a positive aspect as well. The adversity they would experience would also instruct or discipline them in what true obedience was. The prophets used stirring metaphors to express this integral aspect of the judgments. Hosea made it clear that "the Valley of Achor" (dire straits) that they would have to go through would become a "Door of Hope" (Hos 2:14); he also said that Yahweh's striking them was a healing measure as well (6:1, 2). It wouldn't lessen the pain, but it would be effective for thinking new thoughts. Isaiah preferred a purgational metaphor. He spoke of the enemy onslaught to come as a flood that would cleanse away the lies (Isa 8:7–8; 28:16–19), or a fire that would smelt the alloy and extract the dross of Israel's idolatry (Isa 1:25). Jeremiah's most powerful metaphor was surgery. God was like a great physician who would conduct open-heart surgery and suture his Torah onto the collective heart of the people (Jer 34:1–4); since there was no anesthesia, operations were excruciatingly painful, just like the exile. And Ezekiel said that God in the adversity was taking out an old heart of stone and replacing it with a new heart (Ezek 36:26). The horrible pain they were to endure was not an end in itself but a new beginning—if they took it all to heart thereafter (Deuteronomy 29–31).

It was this double interpretation of adversity that pressed the monotheizing process beyond anything it had earlier been. Now the exiles understood that the God who had created and called them in the first place to be his servant people was both their judge and their redeemer: creator, judge, and redeemer, all wrapped into One God. Jeremiah made it clear that Yahweh was creator of the whole world as well as judge and redeemer. In nearly all the passages in which Jeremiah declaimed judgments against the people, he recited God's acts as both creator of the whole world and as savior of Israel from Egypt (e.g., Jer 27:5–7). Further, the Isaiah of the exile offered anthems praising God as creator of all the world and of all peoples (Isa 45:12–31) and yet also as judge and redeemer of Israel. The old story was adaptable for life, expanding and increasing as the process developed.[5]

There would be no going back to polytheism. As Jews, now, they were a people called to be God's servants in the world. So whether they went back to Palestine to live or lived in diaspora, they were to live lives of Torah wherever they would be. They would be God's Torah incarnate (Isa 49:6; 55:4–5; cf. Rom 10:4),

5. Sanders, "The Canonical Process."

as it were. Torah would not be just some scrolls to read and recite (though they would continue to read and recite in order constantly to remember who they were and what they stood for), but Torah was also lives lived as witness to the justice and righteousness of God, a light to the nations by which all peoples could find their way (Isa 2:2–4; Mic 4:1–4).

The name for Yahweh was now to be pronounced with the vowels of the title LORD. Now they would say, "LORD God," instead of "Yahweh God." It was not that Yahweh had grown but that the people through their successive experiences, hard though they were, had come to learn how really big and beyond comprehension God had been all along.

Back in the early days it had been natural for them, both Israelites and Judahites, to think of Yahweh as their national deity. Many peoples believed in henotheism—one major god per people or religion—just like today. Their epic story of escape from Egyptian slavery, wanderings in the desert, and settling in Canaan, all overseen by Yahweh, was not that different from similar epic stories of neighboring peoples and of other peoples of the world. In fact, Amos had said to them that they were like the Ethiopians to God, and that the journeys and migrations of the Philistines and the Syrians had also been Yahweh's doing (Amos 9:7)! The Israelites could not hear that back then. But now, in exile, with new ears to hear and eyes to see, shorn of all God's gifts with nothing to shield them from God's awe-full truth, it was becoming clear that Yahweh God was not just their national god. God was God to all the world.

The exiles recalled that Jeremiah had said something about praying for their enemies and for the city where they had been taken prisoner (Jer 29:7), advice they had thought was sedition and blasphemy. He also said that Nebuchadnezzar, their hated enemy, was God's Servant (Jer 25:9; 27:6)! They thought that too was blasphemy then, but now it began to make sense. And now one of the Isaiah followers in their camp was saying that Cyrus of Persia, who had defeated the Babylonians and liberated them from those prisons after all those years of exile, was actually God's Messiah

Appendix

(Isa 45:1)! This exilic Isaiah argued over and over that Yahweh was far more than Israel's God. This God was the one and only creator of everything that is and, while God indeed had chosen Israel, it was to be a witness to the world of God's way of thinking, God's Torah. Foreigners would come to Zion and Jerusalem, not to invade it now, but to learn Torah, God's will and way for the whole world (Isaiah 40–42; Isa 2:2–3, etc.).

Early Judaism

A colleague, in the same camp in Babylonia perhaps, composed a ringing response to Babylonia's *Enuma Elish*, the account annually recited by Babylonian priests of the creation of the world. It was, among other things, a sort of theogony or mythic account explaining the births and origins of their many gods. The exiles were apparently permitted to go downtown in Babylon and witness the grand parade of the gods during the Akitu Festival, and were undoubtedly impressed with the pageantry. Indeed, some were seduced by it (Isa 46:1–4). The response was what we know as Genesis chapter 1, which recounts the creation of the world in seven days, asserting beyond all doubt that the One God who was creator was the only God that was or is. The writer (scholars say Priestly Source) offered a sort of antitheogony to counter the attraction the Babylonian account had for the exiles, some of whom had perhaps heard it annually for years. In rhythmic cadences and solemn meter Genesis 1 tells of the creation of various items in creation, starting with light in contrast to the darkness of chaos. Most people have since read Genesis 1 as telling the origin of items in creation. And the rabbis thus puzzled over that understanding, realizing that the list of created things in the six days is by no means complete or exhaustive, if indeed it is such a list. To solve the problem, the rabbis posited a time "between the evenings" after the six days when "tongs" (implements or tools) and other such items would have been created in order to get from the list in the six days to where humans actually experience reality.

But that mistakes the real purpose of the Priestly account of creation. If one reviews the list of created things in Genesis 1 in light of the situation in the sixth century BCE in Mesopotamia, one realizes that each item was the symbol of a deity worshiped back in those days. If that is the case, then the chapter, far from being a list of created items, is an antitheogony, composed for the purpose of saying that none of those symbols for various gods had any real meaning for a true cosmology. The Priestly writer starts with God's creating "light" and separating it from the darkness of chaos. The apt student of the text, who reads outside the hermeneutic circle learned in synagogue or church, must perforce ask the question of how light could be created before there were "lights in the firmament," which were not "brought into being" until the fourth day (Gen 1:14–19). If the sun, moon, and stars were all but items in creation, then how could light preexist them? The answer is that they were not simply items in creation. They were symbols of the deities people in Mesopotamia and the Near East generally worshiped in those days. Light was the symbol for the Persian god, Ahura Mazda, Cyrus's principal god! The Priestly writer, a student of the prophets, especially the exilic Isaiah, was saying that light was no god at all. Light was created the same as all the rest of creation, and the exiles about to be liberated did not have to show Cyrus of Persia gratitude by worshiping his god!

And the list goes on, day by creation day in Genesis 1, putting to rest the idea that the heavens were divine, or that fertility in any form was divine, or that the sun represented a deity (as it did in most of the ancient Near East and elsewhere)—or the moon or the stars (symbols of the Pleiades, the Seven Sisters, and other star deities) or the depths of the ocean (where people supposed the chthonian deities or sea monsters held sway) or earthly beings or heavenly beings (Gen 1:20–25). Indeed, earthly and heavenly beings were but fish, creeping things, or birds, and that's all they were—nothing more. There was and is only One God of All; everything else, whatever it might be, is created, including finally humans themselves (Gen 1:14–16).

Appendix

Yahweh was indeed far more than the exiles had thought. In fact, they had learned in exile that s/he was not just their national god. *Yahweh* was the name they had used, yes; but the exiles were learning that there was but one God of all the world—creator as well as judge and redeemer. A god wasn't just for taking care of them. In polytheism and in henotheism a national deity had a reputation to defend. No, God was bigger than humans thought. Far bigger. So much so that the exiles began to experience awe. While so many of the gifts they had been given—like land and temple— were now taken away, nevertheless there was one gift God had given that they still had, and that couldn't be taken away: that was Torah. Torah was God's will for them—the law of God to which all peoples (including kings, priests, and leaders), no matter how powerful, were subject. No foreign army or even natural disaster could destroy Torah the way land and temple had been destroyed. Torah was portable and adaptable for life. It was this aspect of the Jewish epic in its full form that amazed the Greeks to the point that it was the only national epic of a foreign people (Greeks said "barbarian") translated into Greek. And Yahweh was now giving them back the land, but only if they could remember to worship the Giver instead of the gifts he gave them (Deuteronomy 29–31).

Later, after Alexander's conquests, the internationalization of Judaism in the Hellenistic Period reached dimensions no one had thought feasible—so much so, that Judaism was declared by Rome an officially recognized religion. Most Jews apparently did not return to the old sod but chose to stay in Babylonia and became the largest Jewish community in the world for the following twelve centuries. It was there that the official Talmud was codified, not in Judah. Torah had to be adapted in a number of ways to fit to the new situation of individual worth and responsibility. It was in Early Judaism, already under the Persians, that many stories developed about individual heroic young Jews living and serving in foreign lands, who bravely witnessed to their belief in the One God of All: Daniel, Esther, Judith, for example. There were also the stirring stories of bravery in the books of the Maccabees, and many more.

Wisdom literature in general questioned simple views of new problems read solely in the light of old experiences. The book of Job dove deeply into the problem of the excessive individual suffering, and helped to set new guidelines for understanding how the message of the preexilic prophets could be rightly applied in the new situation of Early Judaism. The dialogues between Job and his erstwhile friends (Job 3–31) undoubtedly reflected debates going on in Early Judaism about how to apply preexilic laws and precepts to the new situation of individual worth and responsibility. But how all that was to be understood when Jews were scattered all over the Persian Empire became a real problem. The friends wanted to haul the old laws literally over and dump them onto the head of Job, and Job cried a loud "no" to all such literalism. New precepts had to be worked out, and the Wisdom literature of Ecclesiastes and Proverbs struggled with the problem. Eventually rabbinic Judaism would develop *halachah* (laws) that would apply to individuals and families wherever they might live, and the rabbis made no great attempt to relate them to what was in Torah from the preexilic period. Such halachic efforts eventually grew to become Mishnah, Talmud, and Responsa down to the present day.[6]

A Galilean Sect

But it was a movement out of Early Judaism, indeed one that had first developed in first-century Hellenized Galilee, that exploited the international and universal dimension of Judaism beyond all others and pressed the monotheizing process beyond what it had ever been by focusing on one Jew from the Galilee and what his life and teachings meant. Jesus, the founder of the new Jewish sect, was believed to have lived a life of Torah in its essence (Rom 10:4). He taught that the heart of Judaism was love of the One God of All, and of neighbor (Mark 12:29–34), just as the rabbis were saying. He demonstrated that belief by choosing as disciples a marginal group of Jews from the Galilee. He interpreted Isaiah 61, a favorite

6. Sanders, "The Book of Job and the Origins of Judaism."

passage of Jews of the time, as heralding God's good news for all peoples, not just Jews, by referring to Elijah and Elisha's blessing and being blessed by foreigners (Luke 4:16–30). He chose Roman collaborators, hated tax collectors employed by the Romans, as followers (Matthew and Zachaeus).

Given Jesus's firm belief in God's being the One God of All, in his first sermon, according to Matthew, he even urged his followers to love their enemies (Matt 5:43–48; Luke 6:27–28; cf. Jer 29:7). And then later followers chose Matthew's account of Jesus's life and teaching as the first among four they would keep forever. These accounts told of Jesus's healing whomever was sick, not just the pious. They even told of his healing the "dear servant boy" of a Roman centurion (Matt 8:5–10; Luke 7:1–10), and everybody knew what servant-boys meant to Roman army officers who lived for long periods away from wife and home! Jesus seemed to go out of his way to offend and rile various religious leaders with his open ways and his refusal to follow set custom. He blessed women of ill repute and happily dined with sinners, those scorned by religious leaders (Luke 14:12–24). And all this is recorded in the Gospels, the accounts of his ministry, teaching, and life as the patent reasons he was condemned by both Jewish and Roman magistrates for his unorthodox and seditious teachings. Jesus seemed to condemn what religious leaders (in any generation) hold as proper comportment and custom, and to glorify what they said was wrong to do and say. No outcast in society escaped his blessings—lepers, prostitutes, the crazed, the possessed, Roman collaborators. Women especially were attracted to the movement because it challenged cultural forms of patriarchalism. Is there anyone in today's world who could possibly be outside God's encompassing love? He was and is an embarrassment and a disgrace, every bit as much as the prophets had been in their time, if not more so. Why?

For precisely the same reasons the prophets had been condemned by their contemporaries. Jesus said in nearly everything he taught and did that God was far bigger than what the people or religious establishment believed about God. God, for Jesus, was the God also of those society did not approve of. He even preached that the people society said were shamed in this life were actually those God would honor in the new kingdom he said was coming soon (Matt 5:3–12), and those presently honored would be shamed (Luke 16). That God is the One God of All was his basic message, and he was condemned and crucified for living, talking, and acting like it—just as the prophets had been condemned and threatened with murder for their messages (cf. Jer 11:19, etc.).

All this, indeed his whole ministry, demonstrated Jesus's belief that God was not limited to the parameters and traditions of any religion but was and is the One God of All. Christianity has generally forgotten that, and like all religions has tried to comprehend (contain) God in its doctrines and beliefs, and even to claim exclusive hold and possession of access to God through exclusivist misunderstandings of the incarnation and of the Gospels.

Jesus's early followers came to understand that Jesus somehow represented God her- or himself in a human life on earth. They used earlier Jewish and Greek metaphors such as "son of man" and "son of God" to express that understanding. Eventually they became quite sure that God had been "incarnate" (more of a Greek idea) in Jesus and had come him- or herself to live a human life on earth under the oppression that Jews endured with Roman rule. If God had chosen, in the biblical story, to dwell in the huts and hovels of slaves in Egypt through to their liberation from that yoke, and indeed had sojourned with the Jews in Babylonian prisons until their liberation from that yoke, why might God not have chosen to crouch in the cradle of a Jewish baby threatened by Herod's sword, and have gotten onto a Roman cross suffering all that people suffered under the cruelty of an unchecked superpower accountable to no other on earth? The thing the full biblical gospel makes clear is that God loved and loves humans in an incomprehensibly irrational way, called grace; so it is not beyond thinking that God came among us and suffered what we suffer, showing that human might and cruelty to other humans could not and would not have the last word.

Appendix

The Early Church

The Christian story could not be contained in the Galilee or even in Palestine. Soon after Jesus's death and resurrection (God's demonstration that death does not have the last word, no matter how much it seems like it in human experience), travelers out of the Galilee took the story all over the known world—east and west, north and south—to let everybody know that the One God of All cared that much for them, no matter their tribe or nation (Rom 3:29–30). In the Greco-Roman world, people believed that the end of life was Hades, a shadowy nonexistence in the netherworld. When Odysseus visited Achilles in Hades toward the end of his journey, Achilles told him that he'd rather be a slave in the land of the living than king of all the blind in Hades. That's all even a great hero like Achilles had to look forward to. But these travelers told a different story: the One God of All had just been sighted on the hills of the Galilee in a Jew who taught an amazing message of love and honor for foreigners and even for the lowliest of society. This man had endured all the suffering a human can take, relieved by death, and yet then was raised by God, triumphant above all the miasma of human drama. The story spread like wildfire among slaves, women, and the dispossessed of the world out there.

The followers were persecuted for telling tall tales and disrupting the very bases of society. They claimed that God was judging and subverting the honor/shame syndrome by which nearly all societies were and are structured, and they asserted that Christ was God's *kyrios* for all the world, not the Roman emperor. Each group of Christ followers had different versions of the story, to be sure, but the essentials were basically the same. They were persecuted and reviled just for telling such a story, until the early fourth century when Constantine made his momentous decision to make Christianity the state religion.

With success, of course, come sin and self-deception. The church when liberated—like ancient Israel had centuries earlier, according the prophet Amos—acted like those who had oppressed them, and proceeded to persecute Jews, and later Muslims.

Christians organized into a rigid hierarchy and began to do to Jews and others what Rome had done to them. Christians began to persecute the Jews (and others as well) because they would not fall in line, and so went the way of all flesh. Blessings and honor are and always have been occasion for sin, as both Torah and Jesus taught, and the early Christians proved this rule. The basic story about Jesus got lost in debates over details about who Christ was and how. Right belief became more important for Christians than the simple story when they in turn had power. Christians forgot what Jesus had taught about loving their neighbor, even their enemy. They made concepts of Christ idolatrous and forgot what Jesus taught about God. They forgot that their God was the One God of all people, and Jesus God's anointed for all the world, not just for them and those who believed as they did.

Basic stories about ancient Israel and Early Judaism, including Christianity, were retold and recited often enough to form a group of such accounts that became the Scripture of Judaism and of Early Christianity. It provides snapshots, or rather a montage of freeze-frames, of stories and laws and discussions at many stages, each of which provides a text caught at a different point in the monotheizing process (read synchronically and diachronically) to indicate how Jews and Christians could and should continue the process until they and all the world perceive that God is truly One, and that humanity, made in God's image, is one as well. It provides a path on which to continue to strive—indeed, a sort of paradigm to show how continually to confront reality and the future with integrity and hope in a vision of humanity's eventually coming to realize that, with all its rich diversity, it is one as well. A strong belief in the unity of God clearly indicates belief in the unity and oneness of all humanity. We fully agree, then, with Oxford Professor Karen Armstrong's efforts to stress the similarities of the three Abrahamic religions.[7]

7. Sanders, "The Integrity of Biblical Pluralism." See Armstrong, *A History of God.*

Appendix

The Issue Today

We leave to Jews and Muslims to point out where synagogue and mosque fall short of belief in One God of All. The issue here is whether Christianity can be redeemed, or whether it has become so exclusivist that it is lost in its hundreds of different views of its own identity, each claiming to be the right one. It may be that this is one of the reasons God raised up Islam and many other ancient religions, and has preserved Judaism, so that Christians may be reminded of what Jesus himself taught, especially about the One God of All.

Christians must ask themselves:

- whether their claims to exclusivity do not belie belief in One God (Robert Wright)

- whether they understand the vast difference between henotheism and true monotheism (Karen Armstrong)

- whether any one view of Christ is the only true one

- why churches tend still to be the most segregated institutions in the culture

- why "the other" is often called evil

- why Christians often find war and killing others to be noble

- why the churches tend to uphold whatever culture they find themselves in and sponsor the status quo even when it is oppressive and demonizes those the culture excludes.

Have Christians made distortions of Christ into an idol, in effect displacing God?

Indeed, would a theocentric Christology not be more responsible to Scripture and sound theology than the traditional christocentric theology?

What would a One-God-centered understanding of the Trinity, of Christ and the Holy Spirit truly mean (Douglas F. Ottati)?

The ancient cry *Credo in Unum Deum* has become largely meaningless to those who claim to be Christian today. These are a few of the questions that must be addressed if the church and the earth as we know them are to survive through the twenty-first century.

Bibliography

Akenson, Donald Harman. *Surpassing Wonder: The Invention of the Bible and the Talmuds*. New York: Harcourt, Brace, 1998.

Albertz, Rainer. *A History of Israelite Religion in the Old Testament Period*. 2 vols. Translated by John Bowden. Old Testament Library. Louisville: Westminster John Knox, 1994.

Armstrong, Karen. *A History of God*. New York: Knopf, 1993.

Barr, James. *The Concept of Biblical Theology: An Old Testament Perspective*. Minneapolis: Fortress, 1999.

Brown, Brian Arthur. *Three Testaments: Torah, Gospel, and Quran*. Lanham, MD: Rowman & Littlefield, 2012.

Brown, Peter. *Through the Eye of a Needle: Wealth, the Fall of Rome, and the Making of Christianity in the West, 350–550 AD*. Princeton: Princeton University Press, 2012.

Capetz, Paul. "The First Commandment as a Theological and Ethical Imperative." In *The Ten Commandments: The Reciprocity of Faithfulness*, edited by William P. Brown, 174–92. Library of Theological Ethics. Louisville: Westminster John Knox, 2004.

———. *God: A Brief History*. Facets. Minneapolis: Fortress, 2003.

Dever, William G. *Did God Have a Wife? Archaeology and Folk Religion in Ancient Religion*. Grand Rapids: Eerdmans, 2005.

Downey, Tom. "The Ephemeral City." *Smithsonian Magazine* 44/5 (2013) 63.

Evans, Craig A., and James A. Sanders. *Luke and Scripture: The Function of Sacred Tradition in Luke–Acts*. 1993. Reprinted, Eugene, OR: Wipf & Stock, 2001.

Fishbane, Michael. *Biblical Interpretation in Ancient Israel*. New York: Oxford University Press, 1987.

Goshen-Gottstein, Moshe. "The Psalms Scroll (11Ps[a]): A Problem of Canon and Text." *Textus* 5 (1966) 22–33.

Gustafson, James M. *Ethics from a Theocentric Perspective*. 2 vols. Chicago: University of Chicago Press, 1981–1984.

Bibliography

Hanson, K. C. "'How Honorable!' 'How Shameful!': A Cultural Analysis of Matthew's Makarisms and Reproaches." *Semeia* 68 (1994[96]) 81–111. Online: www.kchanson.com/ARTICLES/mak.html.

Kristeva, Julia. *Desire in Language: A Semiotic Approach to Literature and Art.* European Perspectives. New York: Columbia University Press, 1980.

Lange, Armin, and Esther Eshel. "'The LORD Is One': How Its Meaning Changed." *Biblical Archaeology Review* 39/3 (2013) 58–63, 69.

Leiman, Sid Z. *The Canonization of Hebrew Scripture: The Talmudic and Midrashic Evidence.* Transactions: The Connecticut Academy of Arts and Sciences 47. Hamdon CT: Archon, 1976.

MacDonald, Dennis R. *The Homeric Epics and the Gospel of Mark.* New Haven: Yale University Press, 2000.

MacDonald, Nathan. *Deuteronomy and the Meaning of Monotheism.* Forschungen zum Alten Testament 2/1. Tübingen: Mohr/Siebeck, 2003.

McLaughlin, John L. "Is Amos (Still) among the Wise?" *Journal of Biblical Literature* 133 (2014) 281–303

Niebuhr, H. Richard. *Radical Monotheism and Western Culture: With Supplementary Essays.* Foreword by James M. Gustafson. Library of Theological Ethics. Louisville: Westminster John Knox, 1993.

Noth, Martin. *The History of Israel.* Translated by P. R. Ackroyd. 2nd ed. London: A. & C. Black, 1960.

Oakman, Douglas E. *Jesus, Debt, and the Lord's Prayer.* Eugene, OR: Cascade Books, 2014.

Ottati, Douglas F. *Reforming Protestantism: Christian Commitment in Today's World.* Louisville: Westminster John Knox, 1995.

Rose, Martin. "Names of God in the Old Testament." In *Anchor Bible Dictionary,* edited by David Noel Freedman, 4:1001–11. 6 vols. New York: Doubleday, 1992.

Sanders, James A. "Adaptable for Life: The Nature and Function of Canon." In *Magnalia Dei: The Mighty Acts of God: Essays on the Bible and Archaeology in Memory of G. Ernest Wright,* edited by Frank Moore Cross et al., 531–60. Garden City, NY: Doubleday, 1976.

———. "The Betrayal of Evangelicalism." *Colgate Rochester Crozier Divinity School Bulletin* (Summer 2012) 8–13, 18–22.

———. "The Book of Job and the Origins of Judaism." *Biblical Theology Bulletin* 39 (2009) 60–70.

———. *Canon and Community: A Guide to Canonical Criticism.* Guides to Biblical Scholarship. 1984. Reprinted, Eugene, OR: Wipf & Stock, 2000.

———. "Canon as Dialogue." In *Häresien, Religionshermeneutische Studien zur Konstruktion von Norm und Abweichung,* edited by Irene Pieper et al., 151–67. Reihe Kulte/Kulturen. Munich: Fink, 2003.

———. "The Canonical Process." In *The Cambridge History of Judaism.* Vol. 4, *The Late Roman–Rabbinic Period,* edited by Steven T. Katz, 230–43. Cambridge: Cambridge University Press, 2006.

————. "Cave 11 Surprises and the Question of Canon." *McCormick Quarterly Review* 21 (1968) 284–98.

————. "The Challenge of Fundamentalism: One God and World Peace." *Impact* 19 (1987) 12–30.

————. "The Ethic of Election in Luke's Great Banquet Parable." In *Luke and Scripture*, edited by Craig A. Evans and James A. Sanders, 106–20. 1993. Reprinted, Eugene, OR: Wipf & Stock, 2001.

————. "From Isaiah 61 to Luke 4." In *Luke and Scripture*, edited by Craig A. Evans and James A. Sanders, 46–69. 1993. Reprinted, Eugene, OR: Wipf & Stock, 2001.

————. "From Isaiah 61 to Luke 4." In *Christianity, Judaism and Other Greco-Roman Cults: Studies for Morton Smith at Sixty*, edited by Jacob Neusner, 1:75–106. 4 vols. Studies in Judaism in Late Antiquity 12. Leiden: Brill, 1975.

————. "God Is God." In *Year Book of 1972–73 of the Ecumenical Institute*, 103–27. Jerusalem: Tantur, 1973.

————. "God's Work in the Secular World." *Biblical Theology Bulletin* 37 (2007) 145–52.

————. "A Hermeneutic Fabric: Psalm 118 in Luke's Entrance Narrative." In *Luke and Scripture*, edited by Craig A. Evans and James A. Sanders, 140–53. 1993. Reprinted, Eugene, OR: Wipf & Stock, 2001.

————. "Hermeneutics of True and False Prophecy." In *Canon and Authority: Essays in Old Testament Religion and Theology*, edited by George W. Coats and Burke O. Long, 21–41. Philadelphia: Fortress, 1977.

————. "The Integrity of Biblical Pluralism." In *Not in Heaven: Coherence and Complexity in Biblical Narrative*, edited by Jason P. Rosenblatt and Joseph Sitterson Jr., 154–69. Indiana Studies in Biblical Literature. Bloomington: Indiana University Press, 1991.

————. "Sins, Debts, and Jubilee Release." In *Luke as Scripture*, edited by Craig A. Evans and James A. Sanders, 84–92. 1993. Reprinted, Eugene, OR: Wipf & Stock, 2001.

————. *Torah and Canon*. 1st ed. Philadelphia: Fortress, 1972.

————. *Torah and Canon*. 2nd ed. Eugene OR: Cascade Books, 2005.

Sanders, James A., with Paul E. Capetz. "*Credo in Unum Deum*: A Challenge." *Biblical Theology Bulletin* 39 (2009) 204–13.

Semler, Johann Salomo. *Abhandlung von freier Untersuchung des Canon*. 2nd ed. Halle: Hemmerde, 1771.

Smith, Mark S. *The Early History of God: Yahweh and the Other Deities in Ancient Israel*. 2nd ed. The Biblical Resource Series. Grand Rapids: Eerdmans, 2002.

————. *The Origins of Biblical Monotheism: Israel's Polytheistic Background and the Ugaritic Texts*. New York: Oxford University Press, 2001.

Tomasi di Lampedusa, Giuseppe. *Il Gattopardo (The Leopard)*. Biblioteca di letteratura. I contemporanei 4. Milan: Feltrinelli, 1958.

Terrien, Samuel. "Amos and Wisdom." In *Israel's Prophetic Heritage: Essays in Honor of James Muilenburg*, edited by Bernhard W. Anderson and Walter Harrelson, 108–15. New York: Harper, 1962.

Ulrich, Eugene. "The Notion and Definition of Canon." In *The Canon Debate*, edited by Lee Martin McDonald and James A. Sanders, 21–35. Peabody, MA: Hendrickson, 2002.

Wacholder, Ben-Zion. *Dawn of Qumran: The Sectarian Torah and the Teacher of Righteousness*. Monographs of the Hebrew Union College 8. Cincinnati: Hebrew Union College Press, 1983.

Weis, Richard D., and David M. Carr, eds. *A Gift of God in Due Season: Essays on Scripture and Community in Honor of James A. Sanders*. Journal for the Study of the Old Testament Supplement 225. Sheffield: Sheffield Academic, 1996.

Wright, Robert. *The Evolution of God*. New York: Little, Brown, 2009.

———. "One World, Under God." *The Atlantic*, April 2009, 38–53.

Scripture Index

~

Name Index

Name Index